The Essential Roadmap:

Navigating Family Enterprise Sustainability in a Changing World

Fredda Herz Brown, Ph.D.

with Fran Lotery, Ph.D.

Printed in the United States of America

First Edition

Print Edition ISBN: 978-0-578-63789-1

eBook Edition ISBN: 978-0-578-63788-4

Publisher:
Relative Solutions, LLC
24 West Railroad Avenue, Box 289
Tenafly, NJ 07670

www.relative-solutions.com

Table of Contents

Sustaining anything, be it a person or an enterprise, is a step that means much more and goes well beyond simply evolving. When applied to enterprising families, sustainability involves a purposeful, thoughtful examination of "if and how" a family wants to move forward.

As a concept, sustainability is helpful and useful for any family. But in the case of enterprising families, family units that share resources and assets, it is beyond valuable—it is essential. Sustainability involves a set of practices that are interrelated and can be developed along five essential dimensions. Those practices call for the family unit to think and look beyond simply surviving in this generation or the next, but to think holistically about future generations and what they will need in order to thrive. It is a concept that was first brought to our attention by the UN ... and has since grown in focus and interest globally.

My colleague and friend, Fran Lotery and I first began to think about sustainability while working with clients at Relative Solutions. Together we developed the first version of our thinking about a sustainability model and the concomitant assessment tool. We always expected that our model would evolve as families changed and became more interested in utilizing our framework. It did, and this book represents an evolved version of the model.

The first book, *The Family Wealth Sustainability Toolkit: The Manual*, was written in a spirit of true joint authorship, where we were listed alphabetically, as is the custom for shared authorship among equals. We toiled equally over the ideas and the words! While Fran has certainly continued to serve as a collaborator, sharing thoughts and, at times, assisting in the clarification of ideas, her role is less a "joint author" in this version. Fran has served as a "with" in this revised version, offering wise insights and thoughts. For her willingness to step outside her retirement to do so, I am grateful.

And I remain thankful to have our relationship, which continues to be sustainable! It has been one of the most central, enduring and resilient aspects of my professional and personal life.

The current book is the result of my effort to present a perspective on all the things that have changed since that first book and to present how families can use a sustainability model not only today but also into the future. But while the book draws on some of the ideas in the Manual, it is not intended as a refresher or second edition but instead to stand on its own. It was always our expectation that the model for sustainability would progress as families changed.

While certain aspects of our sustainability model have proven remarkably resilient and as suitable today as when they were first introduced, other areas (such as the changing family demographics, the rise of the information age and the global economy) have evolved. The concept of resilience has been introduced to help families think about what it takes to deal with rapidly changing and challenging contexts. The new edition also explores the idea of scarcity and abundance and its influence on the family's ability to be generous toward others and to demonstrate gratitude.

As these ideas have been added and integrated, the original dimensions of sustainability have become fuller and richer. This has happened in part because of what families have brought to the model in their work, elaborating and expanding the original ideas. It has also happened because colleagues at Relative Solutions—Carolyn Greenspon, Rebecca Meyer and others, like David Harland our colleague in Australia—continue to develop and refine their ideas and creativity in working with client families. To these individuals I owe a debt of gratitude. I anticipate that Carolyn, Rebecca and others will help to evolve the framework going forward.

To Karen Pursley, the Relative Solutions administrator, a big thanks for all her help with the book and with the companion tool. And to Gregory Roll and Robert Rosenberg, who helped me to organize thoughts and present them in a more cogent way, a big debt of gratitude.

Most of all, my gratitude for generosity of spirit, commitment and our joint time goes to Peter Klausner. This long road has been paved by his goodwill.

Introduction

This is a book about building sustainable and resilient family enterprises—measured not in quarters, years or even decades, but in generations.

This book is about enterprising families and the challenges and issues they face in sustaining shared economic interests. It is a book about generations, about founders and their successors, about parents and their children, about siblings and extended relatives, about the tribes and clans that are a consequence of families growing and evolving. It is a book about the responsibilities of ownership—and money—and the complexities that come with it. It is a book about the ties that bind— the financial and emotional attachments that individuals have to one another and to the things they jointly own.

There are many different definitions of what constitutes an enterprising family. Simply put, we define the concept as follows: An enterprising family is an economic and familial unit bound together by kinship and a systematic and purposeful business activity. A family enterprise derives its identity and purpose in a twofold manner: its members are derived from a common stock who share in a common economic organization.

The Russian novelist Tolstoy wrote that all happy families are alike, and unhappy families are each unhappy in their own way. While enterprising families share certain characteristics and evolutionary stages (and we do talk about them as a group), it is critical to recognize they are different from each other and different from other families without shared ownership.

Like any family, enterprising families share a history and connection that arose over time. Prior to the start of the enterprise, they were typical, regular families; the idea of starting a business may have begun with the entrepreneurial vision of the founder and then evolved into something much greater.

To understand how an enterprising family operates and the interrelationships of independence, multiple generations, gender and emotions, you must look to its emotional history. That shared emotional history produces patterns that become so deeply imbedded that the family must work to identify them. Knowing and taking into account past differences can assist the family by anticipating "hot" areas and establishing governance structures and mechanisms to help them navigate the future.

A set of extensive changes in the family between the second and third generations usually heralds the beginning of the complexity for families. By the third generation, enterprising families face the challenge of greater diversity—culturally, geographically (with members becoming more spread out) and even generationally (with it not unusual for cousins ten to twenty years apart to share the same generation). Much like a business evolves from a "mom and pop store" to an organization requiring systemization to get things done, so does a multigenerational enterprising family need to establish mechanisms and structures to help it make the decisions necessary for maintaining growth and achieving sustainability in the future.

Because enterprising families are so interconnected, transitions can become thorny and convoluted, whether the transitions are about the shared assets or related to lifecycle matters. Given the many ways in which the individuals are stakeholders and interconnected, the risks and opportunities associated with any transition can seem staggering.

Marriage typically involves the joining together of two people and two families. But in the case of families with shared assets, marriage is all the more complex. And independence for any young person can be difficult to achieve under any circumstances, but when money and the family are connected, the task becomes that much more complicated. And marriage often means defining membership vis-à-vis the family's assets.

Adding to the complexity is the fact that the business world has itself become more complicated and faster moving. The greatest challenge facing all enterprising families now lies in preparing senior management and the next generation for dealing with change and complexity.

Sustainability and Resilience
Sustainability and resilience together provide a coherent framework for not only managing the challenges arising from complexity but actually pursuing growth. In talking about sustainability, we are using the term in a way similar to its definition by the UN: It is meeting the needs of the present without compromising the ability of future generations to meet their own needs.

Sustainability goes beyond one generation and looks into the future. If desired, it requires practices or behaviors along multiple dimensions to achieve it and the ability to make sharp rights and lefts when the plan is not working. It provides structures for the increasing number of members in a family to operate together, if they so decide, and yet to maintain their individuality. It calls for developing structures to give voice to different constituencies and their concerns, putting in place methods for decision-making, and setting up mechanisms, policies and agreements to deal with the processes for managing change.

Sustainability means thinking about developing the human assets of the family—the intellectual, emotional and spiritual capital, not just business and financial assets. It involves creating systems to educate current and future generations as well as knowing when the plan needs to be adapted or adjusted.

Sustainability sets a foundation and plots out a roadmap for moving ahead, but something more is needed: that "something" is resilience, which is the idea of strength and resourcefulness in the face of adversity and challenges. Resilience is the ability to bounce back and beyond—and to be better off for doing so. Resilience allows for change without impacting the family's core identity, its basic values and mission. It is like a muscle, one that needs to be developed if the enterprising family hopes to sustain itself for generations to come.

Finally, this book is about the journey that began decades ago when my colleagues and I began working with these exceptional families to develop strategies for success. In that time, we have been fortunate in having worked with and learned from these families, each unique in their own way, on their journey towards sustainability and resilience.

I entered the field from the emotional or familial system side. What struck me early on was how the joining of a family and an economy impacted a family's emotional life and vice versa.

Working with families to develop practices increases their ability to journey on successfully. This entails helping families with leadership development, educating the next generation for responsibility and separating expectation from entitlement. It involves the development of practices in governance, connection, accountability and more.

Recently the need to plan was confirmed on a videoconference with two multigenerational enterprising families. One family has 230 family members and 150 shareholders; the other is transitioning from the second to the third generation and beginning to think about what lies ahead. The representative of the bigger family offered the following advice: "The worst thing one can do is to not put forward a plan and strategy for the future. Moving forward is not possible without a plan."

We at Relative Solutions have worked with these families for more than a combined eighty years. Everything in this book is what clients have taught us in case after case.* We recognize, however, that moving towards sustainability and resilience is a journey that not all families are prepared to undertake. We do not tell them what to do. Instead, we offer them a perspective and a framework.

In these pages, you will learn about the many ways in which these unique families have evolved, beginning with the founders and the following generations.

You will learn how a thoughtful approach to the joining of an economy to a family can provide for an immense richness in life.

* In recent years there has been a new kind of wealth generated globally. This wealth arises from the technology sector, and while it is clearly of interest, it is not the focus of this book. Wealth for these individuals, such as Bill Gates, Mark Zuckerberg, Larry Ellison and others, is in the founder stage. Their companies are publicly held, (which has for the most part generated the wealth) in contrast to the privately held enterprises with whom we have had the majority of our experience. In addition, these enterprises have not moved beyond the founder generation, and how that founder's ownership and/or wealth is passed is not completely clear in all cases. We admire the commitment to philanthropy that many of these people have made. However, since we have not worked with a large enough sample of these families, we can only hope that many of the challenges we address in this book will enlighten them as they expand generationally. In time, we hope to complete some research on their decisions and journeys toward sustainability.

■ ■ ■

Achieving Sustainability:
The Challenges, Opportunities
and Complexities of
Enterprising Families

The crossover between a family's emotional and economic systems produces some unique characteristics. These features create some challenges and opportunities not found alone in either system. And because there are no easy, "right" answers to those challenges, it is critically important to understand and balance the needs of the family's economic and emotional systems in devising solutions.

We, and the families we serve, recognize that while it may be advantageous from a financial perspective for an enterprising family to stay together over generations, doing so may not be beneficial for personal or emotional reasons. There are costs for staying together, both for the family as a whole and for its individual members.

At the same time, however, there are many benefits in sustaining the family enterprise, some of which are tangible; others that are intangible. There is an honor and pride that comes from maintaining the tradition of the family enterprise. Enterprising families commit themselves to managing and creatively navigating the complexities of their system. They have developed approaches to maintaining the well-being of the family and its holdings. Such families tend to view themselves not simply as owning an enterprise, but rather as building a portfolio of assets, with the potential to enhance all stakeholders intellectually, emotionally, and socially, as well as financially.

At heart, families who share economic interests must also share and artfully manage these unique characteristics:

- Long-term, shared emotional history
- Tight boundaries
- Extensive membership issues
- Complicated transitions
- A tendency to triangulate
- "Public" family dynamics

Managing these characteristics is the centerpiece for developing a sustainable process for success across generations. So before moving on to the concept of sustainability, we first need to discuss each feature.

Long-Term, Shared Emotional History

While many characteristics are unique to enterprising families, one quality in particular that sets them apart from other enterprises is a long-term, shared emotional history.

Now, one could say that all families have long-term, shared emotional histories. And certainly, that is so. But this feature gets much more complicated when family members also share something together—whether it be a company, assets, or family office—outside of their personal relationships.

With long-term, shared emotional history comes a different set of attachments and connections. Whereas in other families, children ultimately go off to begin families of their own and stake out their own paths, the members of multigenerational enterprising families remain tethered in some manner to the enterprise and to each other, in many cases for their entire lives.

Another aspect of family members with a long-term, shared emotional history is that they tend to exhibit repetitive patterns in how they deal with certain subjects and issues. These patterns extend beyond immediate relatives, such as siblings. So that even for members who have not grown up in the same household—cousins or second cousins, for example—long-term patterns get built into and around the various family branches and how those branches relate to each other. The patterns can influence and mold relationships within the family—often without their even being aware of them.

An example of this issue of long-term, shared emotional history came up in a recent meeting with a family. In this instance, the husband and wife happened to be talking about their four children. One of them tended to be more vocal and outspoken than the other three, something that led to disjunction at every family meeting. This child (now an adult) would get up at each gathering and raise issues she considered important—and then would become upset if matters weren't dealt with in her way.

In the course of our conversation, it became clear that something similar had gone on in the husband's family between him and his brother. The brother would cause upset each time they got together.

Eventually these outbursts between the two brothers (and the rest of the family) led to a decision for the brother to separate himself from the family's real estate holdings. But as I listened to him talk, first about his adult child and then his brother, I realized that the same pattern had also been present in his description of his mother, who had also been a person who "spoke her mind," as he said. The repetition of roles and patterns also makes it a challenge for families to go beyond what was used before. Moreover, ignoring the ones who raise the questions/issues may also impede progress.

Vignette: The James Family Enterprise

The James family enterprise was struggling with defining a joint sense of mission and purpose for the family firm started by their grandfather.

The eighteen cousins—two of whom worked in the third-generation enterprise and three of whom were leaders of the family investment company—were the offspring of four brothers and a sister who had seemed close. When interviewed, a number of cousins expressed their long-standing feelings of rivalry and sense of exclusion from the family enterprise and investment firm. As it turned out, only the children of the two eldest brothers were working in the enterprise. These two older siblings were not aware of the rivalry between the children of the other branches until the cousins in one branch, citing their lack of interest and involvement, suddenly demanded to be bought out.

While the family may have thought it was operating together, it clearly did not understand how tensions festering underneath the surface were affecting its members, its view of the family enterprise and the decisions that were being made. The family was somewhat blind to the underlying patterns that were part of its shared emotional history.

Because these areas have so much to do with sharing assets/resources, we have found that enterprising families benefit from examining patterns around four specific areas: How they exercise leadership; how they handle gender differences; how they deal with money, and decisions about it; and how they handle power and control.

These kinds of long-term relationship patterns, which can carry over from one generation to the next, have an impact on the family's economy. Thus, we must keep in mind two important ideas.

First, the past is always present. Patterns and issues that do not get resolved in the past—when they first appear—tend to be replayed in the present. In the case above, the pattern of a family member expressing an opinion in opposition to the rest of the family repeated itself in each generation. In the case of another family, a father who had an angry falling-out with his brother in a business venture was vigilant about wanting his sons to get along when they worked together. Yet, partly because he kept his sons in lockstep and always focused on their similarity in view, his sons ended up arguing over the very thing he had quarreled with his brother over—namely, the direction of the enterprise and who would be in charge.

Secondly, in working with enterprising families, having an evolutionary organizational chart of the family is invaluable. A genogram/family diagram serves as a kind of guide to the underlying issues. By mapping the family's history and emotional connections for at least three generations, we can begin to see what patterns are repeated and how. In creating the genogram, the family's relationships and its emotional connections between and across generations become clear.

The figure below is an example of family diagram that we either ask families to complete or we complete with their participation.* The boxes represent males; the circles represent females. Names and ages of each family member go in each circle or box. The horizontal line represents marriages, and the children from the marriage are listed in vertical lines joined to the marriage line of the parents, beginning with the oldest to the left. A double line through a marriage line indicates a divorce, and an X in a box or circle represents the death of the person. The genogram can also accommodate information about business roles and ownership of various family enterprises, such as using a double-lined circle or double-lined square to indicate that the family member is employed by the family enterprise.

When one first looks at the family genogram, questions such as these can be appropriately addressed: Who is in the family? What have been the central challenges for this family in moving through time? How do they handle money decisions? Who is aligned with whom and around what issues?

A genogram is a guide both to the family itself and to its advisors. We will go into greater detail about how to develop a genogram later in the book.

Tight Boundaries, Inside and Out

Another quality of enterprising families is the tendency to draw tight boundaries around itself and, sometimes, between its members. This penchant for maintaining borders reflects a set of practical concerns, as well as personal ones: enterprising families often need to maintain a tight rein over knowledge concerning their internal mechanisms, as a slipup can affect an enterprise or foundation.

Paradoxically, even as the enterprising family is erecting fortifications against the outside world, the family exists, to a greater or lesser extent, in the public domain: like it or not, it is always operating inside a fishbowl.

Sometimes, that is literally the case.

Sample Genogram

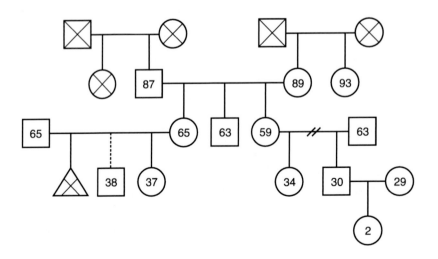

Achieving Sustainability: The Challenges. Opportunities and Complexities of Enterprising Families

1.5

One of the first client families of Relative Solutions had a glass-enclosed conference room, which they considered to be "separate" from their office. In that room, where regular meetings would occur between working family members, fights would erupt, with frequent yelling, screaming, gesticulating and even cursing. Every person who worked for them could walk past the room and could see exactly what was happening, even if they could not make out the exact words spoken. Other employees would know to avoid the family members for hours after these meetings.

Not only would this occur in the course of their everyday business, it would also happen every time we met in consultation with them. We finally suggested that we stop meeting in that room since their family's boundaries were open for all to view.

Another family that we worked with is based in a very small community and happens to be one of the area's largest employers. Whenever they go out to dinner at a restaurant, they have to be ultracautious in their conversation because the waitstaff at most of the restaurants (some of whom have family employed by our clients) may report to employed family members on what they overheard, how they behaved, who had too much to drink, etc.

It's understandable then that enterprising families are apprehensive and often erect walls around themselves.

But such walls, while protective, can also have a negative impact. Enterprising families can become so concerned with the issue of privacy that it can work to their detriment. There have been a number of client situations where tight boundaries have stopped families from seeking out information on how their company is doing, as compared to other companies, because they don't want any information about them to get out. The result is a lack of benchmarks and a hampered ability to learn from mistakes.

Finally, tight boundaries can also exist within the family itself. Very often the members of an enterprising family are connected to each other in every aspect of life: They go to work together every day. Some of them may live in the same household. They see each other for Sunday dinner. They receive their paychecks from family resources, in fact sometimes from one member of the family who controls the disbursements, while a second one reviews their performance, and a third decides on what their compensation should be.

With such connectedness, it's not unusual for family members to draw some artificial boundaries between themselves and the rest of their extended family.

Thus, setting boundaries in enterprising families is important, but defining how those boundaries function is equally so.

Complicated Memberships

Typically, families experience growth and the arrival of new members via marriage, adoption and new births. But those events, which are part and parcel of normal life, signify something very different and more complex for families with shared assets, since they demand looking at the various roles that people may play within the enterprise.

For instance, when someone marries into a family, he or she meets the in-laws first and then learn about the extended family and how to operate within it. But marrying into an enterprising family adds an additional layer to the entrance process, and nothing quite prepares you for life within it. Orienting oneself to the family economy, learning its parts and how they function together, takes additional attention. Such challenges often extend beyond the point of entry into the family.

The normal challenges of familial membership were greatly magnified for John, the man described in the vignette below. He had to figure out how to relate to the family beyond just his relationship with his in-laws. Since many of the economic decisions he and his wife made depended on the broader family resources, it was important for him to understand the details of that group. This was a case in which the family learned from the feedback and developed a set of guidelines and an introductory process to their family "assemblies," both for young family members joining for the first time and for people marrying in.

Vignette: The Grey Clan

John was a fifty-four-year-old man married to a woman whose family had a very large family enterprise. This is how he described his entrance into the family and inclusion in its processes over the years.

"I came to my wife's family almost twenty years ago; we now have three children who are almost at college age. I've had a successful career as a physician-researcher. I have very much enjoyed and learned from my involvement with the Grey clan [his wife's family] and feel very appreciative of what they have offered me over the years in terms of vacations and trips, and educational and financial opportunities. My kids have been given opportunities that I never had growing up, ones that I might not have been able to provide for them. However, I am continuously struck by the fact that I have never been asked to share what I do with the family and have never been invited to share what my family heritage is about. Mind you, it is not that I feel like I am demeaned—more like unimportant. In addition, with so much involvement in my wife's family activities, I have little time to visit my family or have my kids share in that. My wife's family is all-consuming, and I find it difficult to explain my own family's economic means to my children who, of course, would rather go on great vacations than visit out West with my parents and siblings. It is a hard balance to strike, and I think my in-laws view the positives of what they offer without considering the challenges of marrying into this family."

Some families allow a potential new family member to come to some meetings when they have begun dating seriously; others require an agreement that the persons be engaged before bringing them into the fold; and still others require that the couple marry first. There are no right or wrong answers, and the answers must fit the family culture and may change as the family circumstances evolve.

Some families monitor their boundaries further and are highly specific about what information is made available when. They may not expose the new in-law to certain family information when the individual first enters the fold but instead wait until they've taken the full measure of the person. And for some enterprising families, the strong sense of connection to their assets or name makes it almost impossible to allow others in.

To avoid this kind of unwelcome surprise, it's important to treat the prenuptial agreement as involving both parties, and not just as a way to protect one person and their holdings. If the family wants to make use of prenups, then it should provide a relevant framework for younger family members and for those joining it. It is important that they understand how each family views agreements regarding marriage and shared assets.

Vignette: A Prenuptial Agreement

Gene Brown, age thirty-two, was marrying for the first time. He'd worked since college graduation and had just completed an MBA. He'd met his fiancée, Olivia, through work, and they'd been living together for a year.

She had gotten to know his family and relatives and was aware that Gene came from a wealthy family. She, herself, was the product of an upper-middle-class household: She'd always worked hard and made an excellent income.

Three months before their wedding, his parents informed him that the family's attorneys wanted his fiancée to sign a prenuptial agreement so that the family assets would be protected. When he asked, "Protected from what?" he was told,

"A potential divorce." For him, this was hardly the time to be thinking of divorce. He'd never spoken with Olivia about the family's assets, which he tended not to view as his own. When his parents said he should talk with her about it and suggested the lawyer accompany him, Gene thought that was a good idea. Olivia's reaction, however, was very different: She was taken aback, and felt as if she was being asked to pass an entrance exam into a family that considered her a lesser person and did not trust her.

Another aspect of these membership issues involves personal conversations that any young couple needs to have around money. In many marriages, there is often little talk about money. But in those unions where the couple enters with separate assets, there ought to be discussion regarding finances.

Beyond prenuptial agreements, families might want to prepare guidelines regarding the broader participation of new members in family meetings and jointly owned assets. Additionally, enterprising families can develop a process for orienting new members to their mission, vision, and values—just as they do for young family members as they come of age.

Some of our clients call the process a "meet and greet": It's not only an orientation for the new members to get to know the family, but also an effort to get to know the newcomers, too. Some families assign "buddies," not the partner, to new members to answer questions and get to know the new member's particular capabilities, interests, and availability. After learning the basics, the new member is introduced to governance and the family's educational and philanthropic programs or initiatives. There is also time put aside for new family members to introduce themselves directly to the family in a personal way.

The same issues surrounding the incorporation of new members via marriage extend to younger family members as well. When a child comes into the family and grows up, not only do they need to know about other family members, but also about the family's holdings either through trusts, which often have been set up for them, or through understanding how the enterprise and/or family office operates. It becomes an important aspect of their education. At the same time, it is equally important to the enterprising family to have a rising generation on which to build its human capital, given the challenge that human capital can become to multigenerational family enterprises.

While each family needs to define their guidelines for the relationship of in-laws to the family enterprise, we have found that the more inclusive a family is towards new members, and the clearer they are in terms of a timeline and expectations for participation, the better it is for everyone. Conversely, the more exclusive and difficult a family makes it for outsiders, the greater the resentment and animosity will be. Whatever the final choice, it should not be left to chance.

The flipside of giving thought to inclusion and entry into the family enterprise is that it also prompts thought about managing exits from the enterprise. This will be important when someone no longer wishes to belong to the collective whole and the rules that govern them.

As family enterprises evolve, the overlap between family, economy, and ownership begins to move further apart. Initially, these three things were embodied in a single founder, but as the family extends further and further from the founder, those circles begin to pull apart. And suddenly, the enterprising family must examine what are the ties are that bind them together.

Complicated Transitions

Along with extensive membership issues, enterprise and lifecycle transitions are increasingly becoming more and more complicated for enterprising families. This is partly a reflection of underlying demographic shifts: people are living longer, remaining active and vital into older age and thus staying involved in their enterprises longer. In addition, the next generation are often financially dependent longer and seem to be interested earlier in making an impact. As a result, transitions are becoming more drawn out and complex. Instead of two generations involved in the family holdings at any given time—one passing the reins to the next upon retirement—there are often now three.

Moreover, transformative changes are taking place in the general economy, across every sector. Such changes have a great impact on enterprise families. Owners of legacy enterprises can be more focused on the past than on what is currently happening in their industry and what lies ahead. They tend to give too much thought to preserving their legacy and too little to how to transition into the future.

Further complicating matters is the fact that many of our clients are living past the age of ninety. That means that there is greater potential for aging challenges, such as incapacitation due to dementia or to illness. How does one manage an aged family member who is used to having a say in the enterprise? What sort of guidelines should be followed in that case? Such questions are unique to the enterprising family.

On the opposite end of the spectrum, we are finding that young people tend to remain dependent on their families for a longer time than in the past. Achieving a sense of independence is a tough task for any young person, but when money and the family are connected, it becomes even more complicated. Making the transition to adulthood, where social norms dictate the ability to be independent of family finances, can be filled with trials and tribulations.

Recently, a family we were working with identified that several of the industries they were involved in were undergoing major tectonic shifts. They needed to assess whether the return on investment in those legacy industries justified continued investment. It was an issue that deeply concerned the next generation of the family. After much discussion and soul searching, as well as an in-depth analysis, they decided to sell off several of the legacy holdings. This would allow them to redefine their vision for the future.

Meanwhile, the family itself was going through a transition, moving from the third to the fourth generation, and was onboarding younger members into the family economy, even as the nature of the enterprise was changing. Many of the fourth generation had grown up thinking they would be involved in the enterprise in the same way that earlier generations had been involved. But now, not only did the fourth generation have to contend with a reorganized enterprise, but also with the fact that no one had consulted them on this important matter.

Vignette: Developing a Sense of Self

Glenn, a twenty-eight-year-old member of a family enterprise, offered the following thoughts about developing a sense of himself amid his family's abundant resources: "Making your own way in the world is hard when you come from a family that has some wealth. All of my friends talk about the other side, how lucky we are, and I don't want to seem spoiled or ungrateful. I know that others find the process of making your way in the world challenging and that we are lucky, but I also feel it is tougher for me in some ways. I have a father and grandfather and other relatives who are so successful that it's hard to find a way to measure how successful I can be—and what would constitute success anyway? When I applied for my first job, it was not clear to me whether I was being hired for what I brought to the table or for my family name and reputation. And to be honest, having extra money from distributions to do things is nice, but it also makes me feel like I'm still a kid. How much do I have to make to be able to be an adult when there is always more?"

The parents of Glenn, the young man described in the above vignette, had been concerned about raising their children with wealth and creating conditions where they could feel independent. They had thought a great deal about how to assist their children in managing the transition to full adulthood.

If his parents could do it all over again, they told us, they probably would not have created a trust for their son that paid out distributions from a young age. Had they known that the family success would have created such name recognition, they might have chosen a name other than their surname for their holding company and family foundation so as to be more anonymous. In this family, estate planning was done three generations ago so as to be tax efficient. Three generations later, Glenn's father wondered if his grandfather would have taken the same route had he known that the members of each successive generation would have to work so hard to become their own persons.

A Tendency to Triangulate

Human relationships tend to triangulate. What does this mean? Triangulation is where two people are unable to handle the differences, tensions and/or have challenges between them and involve a third person to decrease the tension or, alternately, justify their position. In many cases, these triangles are limited to an emotional, personal, or familial issue. In the case of the enterprising family, the triangles tend to have control and power attached to them. And there is a much bigger platform for triangles to take place on.

These triangles develop when tension arises between two people with regard to some issue or other person. Instead of resolving it directly with one another, one or the other or both persons confide in a third party instead. This move not only relieves the immediate tension but also over time creates an alliance with that third party. It also provides a greater sense of comfort or power than being alone.

However, such action does not resolve the original issue and indeed really complicates it. It is easy as an outsider entering the family to become an unwitting participant in a triangle.

Triangulation helps explain these dynamics. At its most basic level, a triangle evolves when two people have feelings or differences about an issue, and, instead of talking directly to or resolving it with one another, one of them confides in a third family member. Having an alliance is often more powerful than being alone, but once the third person is drafted into the interaction, the second person does not know how the first one feels. (See illustration below.)

Such triangles are common in all walks of life but take on a particular intensity in relationships that are emotionally and economically based.

While family members and branches may move in and out of triangles with one another, positions can become fixed over time. Once that happens, it becomes more difficult to move into a new position. And people develop rigid attitudes and behaviors toward one another and towards certain issues, while forgetting the origins of their conflict.

To an outsider with no previous knowledge of the family dynamics or the issues, it is easy to unwittingly become part of such a triangulation. Outsiders can automatically be viewed by family members as taking sides, whether or not the outsider intended it. And family employees or advisers who align with one portion of the family to the exclusion of the other will suffer in their ability to work with the whole family. At the same time, the family suffers, unable to resolve its issues.

Triangulation

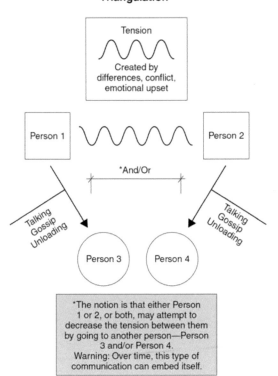

For a consultant, triangulation is like stepping into a minefield where your every action or inaction defines a position, making it hard to maneuver to help resolve a family's issues. We have had the experience of agreeing to do a presentation on what seemed a straightforward subject, like "developing a family council," only to discover that the family was split on the subject. One branch was in support while the other was against the idea, depending on whether they believed their branch would receive adequate representation. Without prior knowledge of this, our position of discussing what a family council was and how it could be useful for the family was viewed as taking sides in a family dynamic. Knowing the family viewpoint on a subject before the presentation would have been most helpful.

Public Family Dynamics

The concept of public family dynamics is related to the idea of boundaries, discussed earlier in the chapter. Whereas earlier we were concerned with the boundaries themselves, here we focus on the dynamic forces that shape those boundaries between the family and the outside world, and how those forces in turn shape how the family portrays itself and its enterprise.

The way in which enterprising families are portrayed in public is not always a matter of choice. A family may want to control the narrative about it, and may even have a plan for doing so, but unless it monitors undercurrents closely, it can't always direct how it's going to be viewed. The broader community will ultimately assign or attribute its own wishes, beliefs, and ideas about the family.

With the territory of being an enterprising family comes the reality that you are in the public eye and that the public believes it has the right to demand things of you. For example, if the family enterprise is situated in a small community, there will be expectations of its involvement in and support of local activities, whether by employing members of the commu-

Vignette: The Carne Family

Larry served as a family office professional for the Carne family for the past ten years and grew to understand the "ins and outs of the family." He had his own view of what went on and believed that one of the brothers, now in his eighties, was the most difficult one and caused most of the difficulties with the other siblings. Larry aligned himself with the majority of the family members in his view of the brother and, though he communicated with that brother and his family, his attitude toward them was not the same as his manner toward the others. He discovered too late that the next generation had witnessed this alignment and decided Larry could no longer serve them in an unbiased way.

ity or by contributing to the community's overall welfare. And the greater the family's impact on the community, its status, wealth, or celebrity, the greater public expectations will be.

The effort to control the narrative is an important part of being an enterprising family. Monitoring public perceptions and dynamics, deciding what your purpose is, and knowing how you want to be perceived is all part of having agency in your own public narrative.

Some families maintain that they are not public at all, when in reality they are. It's inevitable. People view an enterprising family as a single entity, not as a collective of individuals. Thus, any one individual's behavior is reflective of the collective.

For example, in the case of one family with whom we worked, there were several members whose personal finances had been badly damaged. They argued—as did others in the family—that their personal finances were no one else's business but their own and that it was not an issue for the family. However, it became a perception problem. It may even have been a problem for the larger family enterprise, depending on the individual's relationship to the enterprise. There may be bank loan covenants, relating to the family enterprise, that call for them to demonstrate fiduciary responsibility and place limits on personal indebtedness.

Another key aspect of enterprising family dynamics is in giving back to the community. Some younger family members, with lesser financial means due to age than their older relatives, struggle to meet the community expectations of their participation. One of the challenges for successive generations is to "own" that process of giving back in a way that is true to them and not just the result

of what is expected of the collective. It is important to consider how they as individuals, or perhaps as a generation, want to make an impact.

The perception of an enterprising family in the public arena cannot be left to chance—it needs to be thought out, planned for and actively tended to.

Summary

The intersection between a family's emotional system and its economic system produces these unique challenges. Here, the notion of "either/or" is not applicable. There is no one, "right" answer. Instead, every answer or solution must be a balance between the family-system and its economic forces.

Managing these unique features demands a framework which permits the enterprising family to examine the forces at play. Sustainability is that framework.

At its core, sustainability means adapting and evolving. The unique characteristics of a family enterprise can add an additional burden to its plans, so matters must be approached systematically. When a family marries its economic and emotional lives, how does it balance competing needs for independence and connectedness among individuals across generations? How does it define its needs and wants? How does it handle the complex decisions necessary when economics and emotion become intertwined? And, how does it develop the special muscle strength of resiliency to help it maintain a course in the face of setbacks and adversity?

We will address these issues and more in the next chapter. ■

2

Sustainability

In our first chapter, we looked at the unique characteristics of enterprising families and how they face a set of challenges for which there are no easy fixes. Those characteristics need to be managed in a way that enhances, rather than impairs, the capabilities of the family over generations.

Sustainability is the guiding principle here. It allows families to navigate the unique and complex situations that make up their shared journey.

That said, it does not guarantee a family will maintain its success. Rather, it emphasizes that each generation—its talent, assets and intellectual/human capital—must be utilized to its full potential. This is critical in transitioning from the present into the future (in using the word "future" we mean not one, but several generations out).

Sustainability accomplishes two things. For one, it provides a mechanism for planning for the unique complexities of the future. For another, it places one's current needs in perspective. It fosters thought about how to meet one's needs and build capabilities while providing opportunities for building the capabilities of the next generation and those to come.

We define sustainability as it was characterized by the Gro Brundtland; 1987 United Nations World Commission on Environment and Development (WCED) report "Our Common Future." The report stated that mankind "has the ability to make development sustainable to ensure that it meets the needs of the present without compromising the ability of future generations to meet their own needs."

What do we mean by sustainability in the context of multigenerational families? We are referring to the ability of a family to renew and maintain itself across multiple generations if they so choose. We believe that enterprising families have the capacity to create growth that is directed and at the same time is financially, socially and environmentally sustainable.

Another way of thinking about sustainability is that it helps to manage the collective risks and enhances the opportunities of families who share assets. Sustainability involves five dimensions around which families should organize their thinking and actions: Family Legacy and Connection; Governance Structures and Processes; Financial Accountability and Management; Human Capital and Leadership Development; and Generosity and Gratitude.

Sustainability looks beyond one generation. It focuses on transitions over the long term, across multiple generations. And it treats evolution of the enterprise as a choice.

In this sense, it speaks to the notion of generativity, the penultimate phase in psychologist Erik Erikson's theory of human development, a process that he viewed as a journey that all people undertake. Erikson postulated that this stage in one's life journey takes place between the ages of 40 and 65, when adults strive to create or nurture things that will outlast them (often by parenting children or contributing to positive changes that benefit other people). Contributing to society and doing things to benefit future generations are important needs at the generativity versus the stagnation stage of development. Those who are successful at this juncture feel they are contributing to the world by being active in their home and community. Those who fail feel unproductive and uninvolved in the world.

Whereas in Erikson's theory, generativity represents a developmental stage in life, in families that share an economy, the process is that of a journey, which takes place as generations tran-

sition and leadership passes from one age group to another. Generativity, where enterprise families are concerned, means enhancing creativity and encouraging an entrepreneurial mindset. An overemphasis on collective harmony—a lack of tension or conflict—sometimes leads to no change at all.

Sustainability also focuses on the evolutionary changes that occur in all families, particularly between the second and the third generation, when most families tend to grow exponentially and sort themselves by branch.

The addition of a third generation increases the numbers of members who can potentially participate in the family enterprise and the number of family members who are owners but may not want to participate in the enterprise. Extended families no longer tend to live together in close proximity. They live in different geographies and are becoming increasingly global in their interests. Once we are past the sibling generation, family members grow up in different households and have little to no sense of each other's decision-making styles and processes.

Sometimes connection to or knowledge of the founding generation is entirely absent. The sense of legacy and that bond might be diminished. In the case of families who no longer participate in work together, it's diminished even further.

Another key aspect is a focus on strategy. It assumes that the added complexity of family and economy requires coordinated planning: it is not something that can be done on the fly r by the seat of your pants. It demands that amilies have a plan for getting from one place o the other, a roadmap so to speak. It is not simple matter of just living it. You need to now in what areas you have capability/strength nd in what areas you need to develop more apabilities.

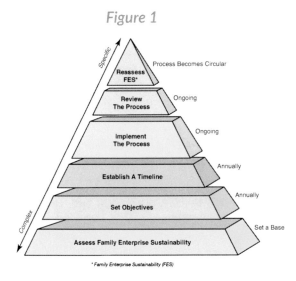

Figure 1

et's turn to each of the five dimensions and heir general connection to sustainability.

The Five Dimensions of Sustainability in Enterprising Families

Family Legacy and Connection

Families tend to think that sustainability is a matter of maintaining the legacy of the enterprises established by the founder, often failing to acknowledge that legacy, like the family itself, is a living thing that must adapt and grow.

There are several areas in which sustainability can address and advance family legacy and connection, all of them touching on the conditions that are necessary for the family to deal with each other on a collective and collaborative basis.

One has to do with purpose. What is our vision? Why are we together at all? What are we doing? What do we want to do together, if anything? People make the assumption that because you're together you need to stay together. This idea of purpose raises the basic question of do we want to remain together— and if so, then for how long?

Vignette: Family Legacy and Connection

The Green family had already experienced the transition between the second and third generation and was now anticipating the transition to the fourth generation. In preparation, the family decided to revisit its existing mission, vision, values, and governance structure. Was it working? The family council decided to survey family members and found that, for the most part, the answer was "yes." However, the family also discovered that the next generation was not as connected to each other or the family legacy as previous generations because they were so far removed from the original family enterprise, which had been sold twenty years before. Additionally, the family clan was increasingly more diverse and geographically dispersed. Concern was expressed that the family wealth would be taken for granted and that there might not be the energy, motivation, or sense of connection to grow wealth that existed in the third generation. Would the vision of the second and third generations to be sustainable continue to be realized if they did not actively pull together around a common vision?

Families at each generational level need to get to know one another, understand one another and learn what to expect from one another. Oftentimes that's done by sharing stories, milestones and having fun together. And it involves moving beyond the lessons of the previous generation (whatever those may have been): Of learning lessons of their own and developing a sense of generational continuity.

Families also need to consider how they communicate with one another, how they go about being together as a family. Learning to collaborate and make decisions together is an important byproduct of spending time together.

Our belief is that while you make a living by what you get, you make a life by what you give. There is a sense of being that comes from participating in a community, that the family itself is a collaborative community. And for most enterprising families, you also tend to serve a larger community, either through providing work settings, or engaging in some kind of impactful philanthropic activities. In order to sustain itself, a family has to have a broader perspective or connection.

There are some advisers, including myself and my colleagues at Relative Solutions, who believe that having strong ways of building ongoing connections instills a desire to build for the future together, of enhancing that which you do well together and improving it for the future.

Governance Structures and Processes

The second dimension has to do with providing structures and processes for managing the unique complexities that face the enterprise family: a roadmap and directions for guiding families on their trip.

A recurring experience we have had in working with multigenerational families is that in the early stages of a family enterprise, the founder usually handles all matters having to do with governance. In fact, more frequently than not we have found that founders are generally uninterested in establishing governance structures and processes since they are from all three circles of influence.

But as families and their joint assets grow, founders often begin to realize the necessity of broad-based, transparent decision-making. At the same time, other family members come to have a voice in governance and in developing structures to help them achieve their objective.

That experience raises a number of questions: What should the board look like? Who should vote and what methods should be followed in reaching decisions? What capabilities should there be in those who serve? At what level does the board serve the family and its holdings? How does the family go about communicating its wishes and wants to the family shareholders? What are the policies and processes that permit a greater number of family members to have access to the joint ownership of assets?

Vignette: Governance Structures and Processes

A third-generation family enterprise was considering whether the time had come to establish a separate organization to handle the family's investments, insurance and other matters. These were becoming too significant a part of the workload for the finance and administrative staff of the family company. In addition, it threatened to become a tax issue for the family. Once the need for the family office was clearly defined, a small family and non-family task force was elected to develop the scope and governance of the office and the job description for the executive. In this case, the family debated for a lengthy time whether there should be a separate board to govern how the family office was operated and finally decided that it would be important to develop a board that looked over all of the family resources. Since there was no family member who had the capacity or the interest to manage the office, the family, when given the options by the task force, voted to seek out a non-family executive. The task force gained family approval, hired a recruitment firm and found an accomplished executive. Along the way, the family became clearer about which decisions they could make on their own and with which ones they needed assistance.

As the family enterprise evolves, the need for board evolves also. Families must develop governance structures that match the complexity of their membership and their assets. There is no one size that fits all. It is not unusual that as families grow, only a minority of its members are actually shareholders, either directly or increasingly more typically through trusts. Thus, the need exists for family board representation or voice as well as the same for the subset of family that are also owners.

So as the size and complexity of the family increases along with their holdings, the need similarly increases to establish guidelines for how it operates. For instance, what are the employment criteria and expectations for family members with regard to all the assets? How will they deal with liquidity needs and exits from assets?

This last item is extremely important. When a lack of clarity regarding exit guidelines is combined with a lack of "voice," there develops a poisonous brew which can lead to litigation and/or severed ties.

There also needs to be a comfort level in making decisions together. An ease in doing so comes from having opportunities for collaboration. As a family reaches the cousins' consortium level, these types of experiences need to be constructed, since the natural circumstances creating them are generally reduced. By the time one gets to the third generation, families have not been living in the same household and thus lack experience in making decisions together.

Of course, there are exceptions to that rule. We have known several families that in the second generation, where you would expect the cousins not to have had that experience, have often lived in close proximity to one another and had very close relationships. So, the members of that second generation of cousins continue to act almost like siblings for at least another generation.

Financial Accountability and Management

A third dimension of sustainability is financial accountability and management. This includes guidelines for oversight, financial responsibility and the continuation of wealth into the future.

When asking seniors in the family enterprise "what keeps you awake at night?", they tend to say that the kids will not be able to manage or adequately exercise oversight with regard to their financial resources. The question is: how to assist the next generation to become responsible "owners" of their resources?

Certain steps can be taken fairly readily, establishing policies and reporting that permit financial oversight in a user-friendly manner. With time comes an education in sharing joint risk and opportunity. Younger family members must learn to participate collaboratively with others.

Yet it is also important that individuals have a sense of separateness to their ownership. There comes a time in the course of their joint life that one or more family members declares the need to define their own risk tolerance in individual investments. This idea often goes in the face of their advisor's sense that having joint investments allows for scale.

Having individual financial ownership tends to increase an individual's sense of responsibility for financial decisions. It gives family members a chance to take responsibility for managing/being accountable for their own fiscal lives. It provides an avenue for obtaining long-term learning through experience and academic expertise.

To ensure sustainability, the next generation must not only "maintain" but build the family financial resources. As families increase in size, the need for financial resources increases. Except in the very wealthiest of families, the need to be able to work/provide a living for oneself is important. It may directly or indirectly increase the family's ability to be sustainable.

Having a roadmap for the continuation of wealth allows a family to move forward in developing a strategic plan to meet their future needs.

Vignette: Financial Accountability and Management

A $150 million family real estate partnership was experiencing a sustained period of stagnation. This had never happened before, and without growth in financial resources, the growing family would have to adjust their risk parameters. At their last meeting, the board members were surprised to hear from a fourth generation, twenty-two-year-old that his sense of the difficulty was not only that the family was not keeping up in the industry but that the family had never seriously considered what ROI they expected from the enterprise and the parameters they were willing to accept to reach that ROI. He redefined the issue as first one for the family and for individuals in it and secondly as an issue for management who needed to develop a strategic plan for getting to that figure.

Human Capital and Leadership Development

The next dimension concerns human capital and leadership development and therefore has everything to do with the intellectual, social, emotional, and spiritual capital of the family.

Family members serve as long-term investors for most family firms, providing patient capital to the economy they share. As time goes on, however, few of the family members tend to work in the family enterprise. Family members need to feel valued and derive a sense of satisfaction from their patient capital. The more family members become investors versus active participants in the enterprise, the more the family must provide for connections in terms of their education and learning. Participating in joint activities that promote development not only increases the total family capital balance sheet but also increases the potential for working and making decisions together.

Not everyone in a family can or wants to be a leader, but everyone does want to make a contribution. The enterprise needs to allow for this through positions for family members to develop their own capacities.

When we focus later on this dimension, we will look more seriously at what goes into developing family leaders. We will examine the mounting research that suggests the importance of emotional intelligence with regard to self, family and others in that process.

A process is required to select, mentor and groom family members to work in the enterprises who demonstrate leadership capabilities and an interest in becoming leaders. In fact, it requires more than just a process. It often requires that part of the process be built into the governance system protocols.

Vignette: Human Capital and Leadership Development

Three young family members decided that after working outside the family enterprise, they wanted to contribute to the enterprise by working within it. Their father and uncle, who were the senior executives of the holding company, were delighted but, thinking their talented offspring wanted to work elsewhere, had never thought about how to deal with entry requirements and tracking performance of family members. They did know it was important that there was a job to apply for and not one made to order for the young person, and they knew that the young person must have the skills and capabilities defined in the job descriptions. They decided that this was a timely discussion for the family to have.

Generosity and Gratitude

The last dimension is generosity and gratitude. In an earlier iteration of our sustainability model and the sustainability tool, we had a dimension called philanthropy, which had a number of items dealing with generosity and giving. However, a number of the families who served as testers of the tool objected to that description, saying that it was a value judgment on our part: Not every family's success or sustainability, they argued, was contingent on a sense of generosity and giving. And some professionals with whom we worked felt the same. However, we decided rather than remove the dimension we would scatter the related items to other dimensions. As we suspected, over time this dimension has been increasingly recognized as important to the long-term sustainability of a family. Thus, these items have once again been given their own dimension.

Generosity encompasses much more than just financial generosity. It has to do with the ability to be generous from the heart—to act from abundance and depth. Gratitude is about being able to recognize and appreciate the many ways that others contribute to our well-being and success. Having a good sense of these two concepts goes a long way to balancing out a belief that one created his/her success on their own and decreases the sense of entitlement that often accompanies that belief.

Enterprising families have a sense of belonging to the social compact that all boats rise together with the tide. They have a sense that Churchill might have been correct in saying that with great wealth comes great responsibility or to those who are given much, much is expected.

There's a tremendous amount of focus nowadays on younger people doing philanthropic work in order to make the world a better place.

The focus on generosity and responsibility has increased, we believe, because the demographics of families are changing. And with the focus on the federal government moving away from its support of social reform, that task has fallen to the private sector, which addresses charitable needs through philanthropy.

This has become a whole new area for families to explore. It can increase family sustainability because it can provide another aspect to their family's purpose. They can pursue a greater purpose, and having that greater purpose may enable them to be more collaborative with one another.

Summary

Sustainability, as we have noted, is a process, not an endpoint. It is a way of thinking about complexity that focuses on building capabilities in five dimensions to permit the family to move forward. Resilience will provide the way of thinking that lets families quickly address changes and learn from disjuncture.

In the end, sustainability gives families the opportunity to develop a strategic plan (see Figure 1), one that balances risks and enhances opportunities that exist when relations share assets together and marry the economic to the emotional aspect of their lives.

In the following chapters, we will dive more deeply into each of these dimensions, and the journeys families have taken on the road towards sustainability. ■

3

Family Legacy and Connection

Sustainability is a journey, not an event. It evolves over time, with transitions and decisions made along the way. Achieving it is complicated—not simply because of the issues particular to individual families, but because combining emotional and economic needs is always difficult. Shaping a family legacy that is formed over time, yet not bound by it, is central to enabling an enterprising family to become sustainable.

Every family has a legacy: the heritage and traditions that are passed along, the values that are modeled, the DNA that is shared. For a family that shares assets, however, legacy is more: legacy is the story of how the family joined its emotional system to its financial one and how this became foundational to people's interrelationships.

While a family's behaviors, values, and emotional life can positively affect the enterprise's economics, they need to be kept in check for their possible negative impact. And though a legacy on the surface may seem inviolable and something that needs to be passed along in toto, the reality is the reverse: for a legacy to endure, it must undergo change. Each generation must modify what's been passed on to it from the earlier generation, whether directly or indirectly. Thus, each generation is uniquely responsible for enhancing the positive sides of the legacy and promoting sustainability.

Inseparably bound are the family's values and culture. These become particularly important as families grow in size and complexity. They form the backdrop for family holdings, philanthropy, and the like. A family should be able to affirm the correspondence (or lack thereof) between its activities and its values.

Formulating the Mission: It's About Family, More Than Financial Assets

The most successful organizations, studies show, share one common thread: all possess a strong yet adaptable culture—an ethos that members of the organization understand, buy into, and take pride in. In the family enterprise, the legacy and narrative is the basis of its culture, evolving and changing in step with the people who define it. But culture doesn't happen by accident: it develops through supervision and nurturing, so that it becomes clear, compelling, demonstrated, and celebrated.

Developing a shared family legacy and narrative is not as simple as it sounds. The word legacy is defined in Old English as "a group of people on a mission." The family legacy is a group of people on a mission to faithfully direct the family's holdings and the conduct of its members. At its best, the family legacy inspires the group and fulfills its individual members who come to see their values reflected in the enterprise.

Values and culture are inseparably bound within a family's legacy as well as its connection to the family enterprise and to each other. It begins with having clarity about those values and culture that guide the family in its pursuits. Values and culture become particularly important as families grow in size and complexity, forming the backdrop for all they do together.

Combining the Mindset of Shared Risk and Shared Opportunity with a Family's Emotional System

The stakeholders in the family enterprise continually shape the family legacy, using it as an investment in their future. While initially the godchild of the entrepreneur founder, legacy quickly becomes an essential part of the family's fabric, its narrative. For long-term prosperity, investment is made through, on behalf of, and in (the development of) family members.

Over time, family members not only share a vision, values and mission, but also risk and opportunity. Shared risk is a key characteristic of a family enterprise. Because of this, families and their individual members need to be more deliberate and explicit about family interactions—how they relate economically to each other, how they make decisions, how they choose leadership, how change occurs, and so

on—all of which may influence their shared economic future and their emotional connectedness. Legacy involves how joint meaning is assigned to the shared economic and emotional life. It is how the family defines its beginnings and how it views its future.

The patterns of family relationships, wittingly or unwittingly, are part of their legacy. They can benefit a family enterprise—or undermine it. But they are inextricably linked.

When family members view themselves as being connected in a real and lasting way, they tend to adopt a long-term perspective on their human and financial capital. The focus turns to the future and determining the right balance of growth and value strategies.

In addition to the long-term perspective on capital, however, there is a need to keep investing in continued growth through entrepreneurialism. Experience has shown that without an entrepreneurial perspective embedded in their values and culture, family enterprises are challenged to successfully support the increasing number of family members. Unless the focus is on growth rather than preservation, the family's expanding numbers and complexity will typically exceed the increase in its assets.

There's a tendency to believe that maintaining a legacy precludes change and adaptation. In such instances, families cling to unsustainable business initiatives because they are bound up in the family's history. An investor mindset can help in assessing the best use of assets. And a family governance process can ensure that different insights and voices are heard. Resilience helps a family deal with both.

Vignette: When Legacy Becomes the End in Itself

A family enterprise that had operated in the United States for almost seventy-five years watched as its market share went into free fall, declining an average of ten percent annually. Nearly everyone in the family was sharing in the business, drawing salaries, dividends, or both. Despite the shift in marketplace demand, the elders in the group resisted changes to the business' focus. Now, the third and fourth generations are grappling with how to keep the enterprise together and reinvent it for today's marketplace.

Along with greater financial resources, new methods are needed to keep the family connected as it grows in number and in diversity of interests and geography. It puts pressure on the clan to embrace this diversity and find ways for family members to appreciate one another, accept their differences and cherish their connections. Not only does a governance structure (a topic we explore in greater detail in Chapter 4), provide for teamwork and decision-making, it serves to help family members get to know each other's capabilities. Importantly, long-term trust is built on experience.

Participation in the family enterprise fosters continuity, connection and legacy, and encourages the development of individual and collective self-esteem. Family members gain a sense of self-worth from their contributions, whatever their scope. At both the macro and micro level, the enterprise benefits from allowances made for ingenuity and informed risk-taking. The focus on participation has the important side effect of developing human capital, from which the family reaps a substantial emotional and economic payoff.

Vignette: Initiating and Inculcating Family Legacy

One family developed a learning/development committee whose task was not only to provide a way for the family members to learn about their legacy, but also to learn about the family and its current holdings. The committee developed an orientation program for all new family members. It then offered courses on finances, developed an investment club, and initiated other opportunities for the family to learn from and to experience together. Thirty family members, drawn from four generations, participated in the program, with the older generation mentoring the younger ones. The younger members later used their experiences as part of the college and job application process.

Adopting a shared social mission can be part of a family's commitment to a defined set of values. A social mission (which we discuss in greater detail as Dimension 5: Generosity and Gratitude) allows family members to see themselves as giving back to the larger community that has supported their success. The strongest family enterprises tend to encourage generosity, gratitude and community involvement, where members can discover the reaffirmation that comes from contributing to the public good. The Rockefeller, Annenberg and Getty families are prime examples of how generosity, gratitude and an engagement with the community (both local and global) can give vitality to the family legacy: those high-profile family enterprises are widely recognized for their extraordinary good works. A social mission and the sense of what it can accomplish can produce a valuable bond among family members, enhancing their emotional connections and partnership in the family enterprise. A family's social mission can also serve as a learning experience, enlarging members' views beyond the limitations of their own self-interest.

Family Connection: More Complex over Time

Legacies tend to bring people together. And strong bonds are a hallmark of high-performing teams—those teams are the ones that people will work hard to belong to. The more high performing the team, the stronger the team bonds become, as each team builds on the other.

Sometimes, however, the bonds become so tight that one feels strangled. Feeling like you are your own person, a true individual, becomes increasingly important in an organization that functions on collectivity. As with most matters related to enterprising families, the issue is complicated.

When families share assets, the continuum that stretches between connectedness and separateness becomes increasingly tenuous. On the one hand, the interpersonal relationships, rather than the shared assets, represent the real source of the family's strength and are what hold it together in the long run. On the other hand, separateness or individuality is also a natural human need. People need to be able to exercise personal choice: Just as employees perform best when they have some control over their work processes, so do the members of a family enterprise.

When family members feel stifled by the ties of connectedness, separateness can become an end in and of itself, thus diminishing family strength. In that case, they may shrink from participating fully in the family, by retreating from family philanthropy, for example, or by filing legal suits demanding greater voice in the enterprise. Families should avoid such conflicts, leaving room for individuality and, as a last resort, by providing pathways for exiting the enterprise.

This balance is particularly critical for younger people who may find it difficult to define their own mark in a world in which they are surrounded by the success and accomplishments of earlier generations. Feeling free to pursue their dreams and to define what motivates them is important to their commitment to the larger family system and to the family as well, since it is in the family's interest to encourage both separateness/sense of independence and entrepreneurialism.

Vignette: Trapped Between Passion and Duty

The Bells were a high-achieving family conscious of its status in the community. The couple had two children, both of whom were very accomplished. Liz studied dance and theater beginning at age four. She continued to be passionate about performing and had visions of becoming a choreographer and working on musicals.

However, she felt compelled to follow in her father's footsteps and to attend his alma mater. He never told her directly that he wanted this, but Liz felt in her heart that he expected it. She did not feel strong enough to tell him she saw herself attending a performing arts program and working toward a career in theater. She loved her father and did not want to seem ungrateful for the life he and her mother had provided her.

So, she majored in economics, and after graduation, went to law school. Although she continued to dance and perform, her studies were demanding, and by the time she graduated and accepted a job offer from a prestigious law firm, she had all but stopped pursuing her passion. Within the first year of being an associate, she knew she was in the wrong place. The only ones happy about her chosen career were her parents. She was conflicted about what to do. More and more, she avoided her parents and withdrew socially as well.

Finally, at the age of twenty-seven, she worked up enough nerve to confess to her parents that she was living their dream, not hers, and that she hoped they would accept her decision to return to her first passion of performance. As it turned out and as she had suspected, her parents were not pleased with her decision and wondered if she would be heading for a life of disappointment and economic struggle. They were also concerned that she would live off her inheritance rather than make her own way. However, they viewed her inheritance as giving her a chance to pursue her passion.

Liz threw herself into dance and theater. She struggled for several years but was committed to eventually covering her expenses through her earned income. And she was never happier. She no longer avoided the family and took a great interest in the family's charitable giving. Through her influence, she was able to draw her family's attention to a project with which she was involved helping underprivileged girls build self-esteem through theater arts. This project became a unifying family activity for many years, providing a way for her parents and family to become involved in a charity that was changing lives.

As multiple generations become involved, connections increase in complexity. Sometimes, as families move past the second generation, an interesting pattern emerges:

The founding generation typically reflected a unity of all aspects of the family and the business, the values, outlook, and even geography. They were not faced with the issue of far-flung family members living in different geographies and different values. Some of these issues only began to arise in the second generation, as the families began to show greater diversity. But even in the second generation, these issues remain relatively simple as compared to the complexity that arises in subsequent generations. However, as a family grows, a clan structure arises, with each branch forming a tribe that functions somewhat independently, defined by its own geography, values and structure, and yet part of the greater whole. The structure allows for separateness—discrete branches, separate households, broader definitions of membership and roles. But at the same time, it poses a challenge: Given the separateness of a branch structure, how can the clan's connectedness be maintained and how can it stay united in purpose?

The pressures to stay connected, yet remain separate, and to manage the anxiety and tension, become more complex. And the opportunity for rivalries or inequalities to develop among the branches also becomes greater. Triangulation—or indirect communication—becomes a greater risk. Polarization among individuals or family tribes and camps can lead to destructive alliances that are passed down from one generation to the next, with the parties often no longer knowing the source of the enmity. But, as we will see, there are methods for dealing with competing interests and other issues that have the potential to weaken the family enterprise.

Marriages, which are a cause for family celebration, can often become a challenge to the balance of family connection. It is difficult to deal with the introduction of new adult members, as they enter the family fully formed, with their own sense of themselves. The arrival of new members at any family occasion can be flashpoints not sufficiently appreciated. Those who marry into any family may feel acceptance issues, whether or not they are part of a family enterprise. The process of getting to know one another is not only based on the twosome but on threesomes, foursomes, and of a whole family taking time and effort.

For families that share assets, the process of integrating new adult members is much more complicated. The new entrants must learn about the family and its holdings. They may see their partners as more "married" to the enterprise than to them. Balancing relationships and defining the role and prerogatives of in-laws becomes a necessity. Some enterprising families set structures for entering or leaving the family enterprise and suggest potential roles—formal or informal—for new husbands or wives in an effort to be inclusive and define the connections.

Even if a new spouse is not actively involved in the enterprise, tensions can arise. A strong family presence can sometimes overshadow an appreciation of a spouse's achievements or reputation, or the enterprising family's demands may interfere with building effective connection to the in-law family that comes with the new spouse. The way that a newcomer is brought into the family and the need for sensitivity in those early interactions should be considered.

Vignette: The Greys

A noted scientific researcher married into the Grey family. The Greys were an established family, devoted to its business enterprise. In most settings, being a researcher would carry status. In this family, such success was not acknowledged. Over the course of twenty years, no one explored what the researcher was doing or asked how his work was going. The family's enterprise, its established connections, and its insular focus all worked against appreciation of a new member. This left the researcher feeling neglected and inadequate, while also preventing the family from reaping the benefits of his contributions.

Family Connection Independent of Sharing Assets

There comes a time in every family enterprise, usually by the third generation, when someone wants out of the shared asset pool. One or more members may feel disengaged or may wish to separate from the clan. They may have some special need or want to pursue a venture independent of the family enterprise. We believe that smart families enable members to change their ownership status as direct or beneficial owners—without guilt—and still remain in good standing in the family. Pruning the tree in terms of family holdings is important and needs to be a part of sustainability planning. Individuals should have the ability to withdraw from economic participation—and to rejoin should they change their mind. Either way, maintaining the emotional connection to the family is in everyone's interest. Simply put, it's good business.

Clearly, family ownership is not the same as family membership. For some families, owner-ship is viewed as an inheritance; in others, as a gift; and in still others, as something to buy. For an increasing number of families, owner-ship is not outright but rather indirect, as beneficiaries of trusts. Each family defines how it is to be viewed, treated and transferred to another generation. In this way, ownership becomes part of the family legacy and shared value. Ownership issues that are not carefully defined and differentiated from family membership can be destructive to the legacy. Accommodating the changing needs of individuals is a key aspect that must be incorporated into the family's legacy. The bottom line: Defining and continuing a legacy calls for attention each step of the way.

In the Samson Brothers Family case study, we introduce you to family members and then follow them throughout the next four chapters. You have the opportunity to witness the family as it evolves over time and faces the challenges posed by each dimension on its path toward sustainability.

Case Study: The Samson Brothers Family

This first installment in the Samson Brothers Family case study provides history and context for the challenges the family faced by examining the first dimension of family wealth sustainability: Family Legacy and Connection.

Family Legacy and Connection

Emmett and Conrad Samson are brothers who bought their first rental apartment buildings in 1950, using their inheritance from their father Carl, and a loan from their mother Emma for the down payment. They worked side-by-side until they separated the apartment management and maintenance division from the development side. Samson Realty was a testament to their hard work and their working relationship.

Each was married, and between them, they had four children. Emmett married a local woman, Jennifer Lang, from a realty brokerage business. Conrad met Jennifer's friend Paula when she was invited for a family dinner. Not long afterward, they were also married, and the two families grew up together, living nearby and raising their kids together. Both wives felt a part of the business, including the initial decision to use the inheritance to buy the first buildings. Both couples felt it was important for their children to have a sense of connection to their cousins.

Education was important to the two families, and the cousins were encouraged and supported while they pursued college educations. Some even went further and earned graduate or professional degrees. They stayed in close contact, frequently traveling together and working together during school breaks. The business was a frequent source of conversation at the dinner tables of both families.

In the late 1970s and into the 1980s, the next generation joined the family enterprise, one by one, as each finished his or her education. Emmett's eldest daughter Jane, who had worked summers in the real estate leasing division, had graduated from law school and served on the in-house legal team for a large real estate company in another city. When she joined the family company three years later at her father and uncle's request, she worked with a long-term and loyal nonfamily executive, Bob Lanry, who headed the leasing area. Bob was asked to mentor Jane and assist her in developing the legal side of the leasing work. His plan was to retire in five years, leaving the department in her steady and capable hands.

As the eldest of Emmett's children, Jane was also the first to marry, and two years into her work with the family real estate company, she married Van. He was an investment banker with strong ties to his family, who lived in another state.

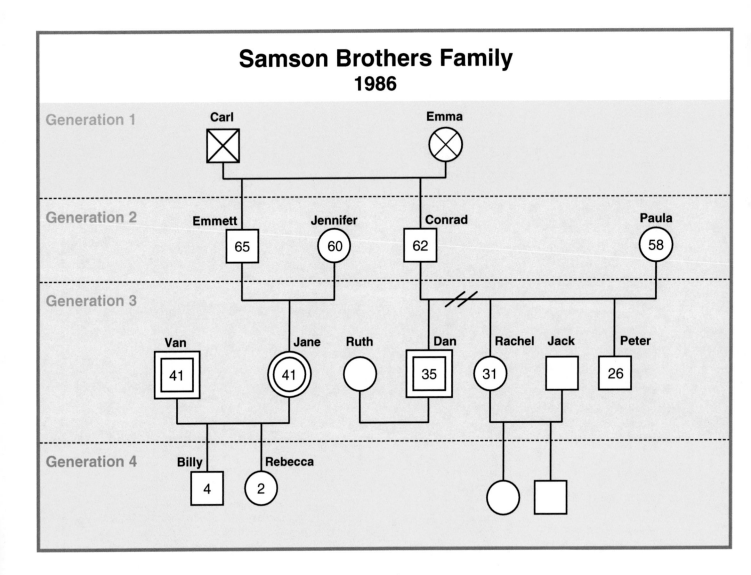

Samson Brothers Family
1986

Generation 1

Carl

Emma

Generation 2

Emmett 65

Jennifer 60

Conrad 62

Paula 58

Generation 3

Van 41

Jane 41

Ruth

Dan 35

Rachel 31

Jack

Peter 26

Generation 4

Billy 4

Rebecca 2

Case Study: The Samson Brothers Family
(Continued)

While he longed to move back to his home state, he also was very proud of the heritage of the Samson family. He thought he could make a contribution to the family enterprise by working with them on the funding and leveraging of their ventures, as well as by dealing with mortgages and tenant financial issues.

Shortly after their marriage, Van asked his father-in-law if he could come to work at the company. Since there were few, if any, explicit rules for how to manage the next generation's entrance into the business, Emmett did what he always had done with decisions: He went to his brother Conrad and asked for his concurrence.

Conrad agreed, but thought in the back of his mind that this was just the beginning! They had both raised their children to be excited about and interested in the family business, and this would be the first of many requests to be a part of that business. In fact, he knew that his oldest son Dan, who was graduating from business school, would soon be asking for a job with the company as well. Thus, doing what he had always done, he agreed with Emmett's request regarding Van, in hopes that Emmett would return the favor in kind when he sought Dan's entrance to the firm. Jane continued to grow in her capability in the leasing division; her father and uncle received glowing reports about her contributions to the business. Jane felt she needed to be included in some of the "bigger picture" issues in the com-

pany regarding the expansion of the holdings and how it should be done. She heard a bit about this effort from Van, but he, too, did not particularly feel that his contributions were well regarded by either Emmett or Conrad.

In 1978, Dan completed his MBA after receiving an undergraduate degree in architecture. He first worked for an urban planning company, exploring issues related to creating mixed-use housing. After three years of building preplanned communities in urban areas, Dan was ready to see how he could assist the family real estate holdings. He approached his father, Conrad, to see if there were any opportunities there. Conrad reached out to his older brother, now almost sixty years old, to get his concurrence. Emmett was quick to say "yes," not only because he always had liked and respected Dan, but also because he thought he had received acceptance of his children in kind. Dan began to work with Van on the funding and banking side of the business. Perhaps because of his background in architecture, Dan was always pointing out buildings he thought the family might find interesting from that perspective.

While the three next-generation family members, two cousins and one in-law, were joining the residential real estate management business, the business blossomed on the commercial side. Conrad, now fifty-eight years old, continued to lead these development efforts. Conrad had a nose for the business and an eye for good real estate

Case Study: The Samson Brothers Family
(Continued)

investments. He led the company into the New York commercial market in the early 1980s to take advantage of an economic downturn. Having always been very financially conservative, Samson Realty was positioned to take on some risk. The company was able to acquire commercial properties inexpensively and limit its leverage during the high-interest-rate era. Van was instrumental in assisting the company in getting new mortgages, and in bank lending and deal making. He was respected by everyone with whom he dealt, and Conrad began to rely on Van's acumen.

Conrad's divorce in 1985 strained the company's financial condition because of the terms of the divorce agreement, which gave Paula a cash settlement and forced the sale of some valued properties. In addition, the financial hit seemed greater because there had been little planning with regard to either brother's estate and to the protection of their current holdings.

Dan had begun to notice that there seemed to be little planning with regard to the ownership of buildings and had shared his concerns with Van. However, nothing was done, and consequently, with the outflow of capital to settle the divorce, Samson Realty's ability to grow became limited. Growth throughout the 1990s slowed within the fairly new commercial area. However, growth was even more hampered on the residential side of

the business because of the high percentage of rent-controlled apartments and limited funds to convert the properties to co-ops and condos.

The intra- and interfamily closeness was impacted by Conrad and Paula's divorce. Jennifer and Paula, who had always been close, now struggled to maintain a relationship in the face of this new family reality. Conrad's children, Dan, Rachel, and Peter, his youngest, were angry about the situation, blaming their father for being inattentive to and distant from their mother. There was talk of Conrad being involved with another woman, a scenario he denied, and of experiencing a midlife crisis.

On the surface, Conrad and Emmett's relationship seemed as solid as ever, but it was clear that the foundation had been rocked. The second generation noticed they weren't spending as much time together and that their decision-making process seemed slower than before. In the family context, Emmett always seemed pulled between wanting to have his brother over for family occasions, while Jennifer wanted and missed her friend, Paula. And Emmett also missed her.

The next generation was increasingly aware that while there were changes in the relationships of the previous generation, their own families were growing. They knew that unless they

Case Study: The Samson Brothers Family
(Continued)

began planning, it was unlikely the business would provide the same opportunities for them or the future generations. Van and Jane now had two children, Billy (age four) and Rebecca (age two). Dan had recently married a young woman he'd met in graduate school. While they did not yet have children, his younger sister Rachel, who had married while he was in graduate school, had two children. Rachel and her husband Jack did not have an interest in the management of the company, but they clearly were going to be owners of the family holdings.

For the Samsons, family legacy was important and ongoing family relationships within and across generations was the norm until it was disrupted by a divorce of one of the family "elders". The divorce not only shook the family expectations about togetherness, it also challenged them to think more about how to stay connected.

The sense of connectedness and legacy, which had sprung up almost effortlessly between the first cousins, would require greater supervision and nurturing if it was to take hold in the third generation. The question of how to create that same connectedness and legacy increasingly began to dominate the thinking of the family.

Summary

Every family has a legacy: the shared heritage, traditions and values that bind its members. For a family that shares assets, however, it is much more: legacy is the story of how the family joined its emotional system to its financial one and how this became the foundation of relationships between members.

For a legacy to endure, it must undergo change. Each generation must modify what's been passed on to it. And each generation is uniquely responsible for enhancing the positive sides of the legacy and promoting sustainability. Shaping the family legacy is central to an enterprising family becoming sustainable.

In the next chapter we will talk about another key element in sustainability: the role of governance. ■

Governance Structures and Processes: Helping Families Achieve Goals

Building an enterprise is an achievement families can take pride in. It takes work and attention, but the payoff can be enormous. In the early stages of a family economy, an implicit hierarchy moves the enterprise forward. But once the enterprising family increases in size and complexity—by the third generation, if not the second—more formal structures are needed to keep the family on track towards achieving its goals.

Governance is the next step, helping organize and nurture an enterprise's roots so that it can flourish under changing conditions. Establishing a structure and policies to organize interpersonal dynamics is a necessary step for families aspiring to sustainability. It provides a framework for resolving problems of trust and connection, formulates explicit and shared agreements about family assets, and defines liquidity and exit options.

Every family unit—even ones that are not enterprises—has an informal, implicit structure for making decisions and policies for working together harmoniously. But families that share assets usually require a more formal, explicit structure to reach decisions, consider opportunities, and deal with risks. Governance helps to manage personal dynamics so they can serve as an ally to the enterprise rather than its greatest nemesis. Governance processes and structures also assist in maintaining five distinct, yet related, functions:

- Oversight of liquid assets: equity markets and bonds
- Oversight of illiquid assets: family owned and/or ownership stakes in operating companies or real estate
- Family connection: developing relationships among family members and sharing a sense of purpose
- Education: increasing the knowledge base and sense of 'ownership' among family members, learning to solve problems and creating a forum for developing trust, and leadership suited to the needs and vision of the family enterprise
- Generosity: creating a sense of gratitude for being a recipient of the family's wealth, and learning about the needs of others and the act and meaning of 'doing good'

Enterprise families are those who have combined their family system to an economic one requiring a mind shift from one that owns a business to one that shares assets accounting for overall family wealth. The more complex the family and its holdings, the more defined the structures and processes need to be so as to evolve and deal with the functions.

Formalizing the governance structure allows members to take responsibility for the family's financial, human and social capital in a more orderly way. It creates a set of guardrails for dealing with various challenges. In this way, the family can codify its decision-making processes—whether decisions should be reached by consensus or majority vote and/or which decisions should be handled in one way over the other. Working together on governance gives members an opportunity to know one another and function as a unit.

Family members may establish specific guidelines for how often they meet, what issues will be discussed, and which constituents will make what decisions. Some families have created family constitutions that outline the principles that guide them. Family members can also address the differing needs of shareholders for liquidity, loans or other benefits. A sub-group, such as a family council or family assembly, can also evolve, delegating some of the family functions to standing committees (such as education and connection, investments and generosity).

Families that have managed to sustain themselves for five or more generations usually have to revisit their governance structures to meet their changing needs. Generally, these families have sought clear, yet sophisticated and flexible governance that enhances positive qualities of building financial and human wealth.

Why is there a need to develop this kind of family infrastructure? The bigger and more complex the family becomes, the greater the potential for differences to arise among its members. Family members at different life stages (or with different approaches to money) may want to invest money differently. Some may wish to seek new businesses to invest in and employ their talent and abilities, while others may want to play a more passive role and have a portfolio of more liquid assets.

A family that hopes to sustain its economic base must be able to accommodate the diverse agendas, needs, and desires of future generations as it makes decisions in the present. Just as investment goals tend to evolve over a lifetime, generations in a family may have longer or shorter horizons in mind. Differing values toward money can also arise as a family grows and its branches are no longer as geographically close or experientially similar.

During the first and second generations of the enterprise, when family is still defined by those who grew up in a house together, it is easier to define what (and how) assets or wealth will be shared. But by the third generation, the ownership group has outgrown the initial, often informal structure. Members from different families may have different stakes and opposing agendas may become entrenched. Siblings may have different numbers of offspring—an only child versus four children—and thus, share unequal financial stakes. Also, legal entities, such as trusts, are frequently used to deal with ownership, creating some potential differences in how various family members view their connection to the economy.

Governance provides a way to make decisions on various issues and to define who makes the decision.

Vignette: Transitioning from Instinct to Governance

One patriarch from a family enterprise had been in charge for a long time, operating primarily on instinct. He couldn't understand why it was important for the family to formalize decision-making and governance. In addition, he had difficulty dealing with the fact that his daughter—a female—was now running the business he had built from the ground up. Though they had always been extremely close, once the roles had shifted, he simply didn't want to listen to or participate in more formal family governance sessions. It took time for him to appreciate the value that an orderly governance process added to managing an increasingly complex enterprise and to accustom himself to his daughter's special skills in dealing with new challenges.

fter the first and second generations, families sually become geographically dispersed and hay have members who need to put their ssets to work in different ways—and may want different relationship to the shared assets. lot everyone is the same: While all may be wners, some may take a more active interest h how the family's wealth is used. Some may vork in the enterprise as executives, managers, r employees; others may serve on the board. mong those who are investors or owners, ome may be spouses, cousins, more distant elatives, or nonfamily members. Generational ples change, transitions take place, and the mily has to confront the challenges of shifting ower and control.

hat growth in numbers can also be a source f strength, such as creating economies of cale for investable assets. But when there are o processes or structures for dealing with ompeting agendas, the challenges can derail n enterprise. Instituting family governance heasures ensures that economic and emotional onds are managed productively and for the ood of all, despite any individual differences. ffective governance systems help to keep he enterprise on track.

Family Mission: The Cornerstone of Governance

So, what is the track, the course, the family has chosen? Attention to governance begins with revisiting a family's vision for itself and its mission. Members should periodically take time to assess their reasons for remaining in business together and should take this opportunity to recommit to or redefine their goals.

We have found in our work with clients that clarifying these goals anew gives the family an opportunity to work together on planning and furthers the interpersonal understanding and relationship-building needed for the enterprise's sustainability. This can be especially important in a period of transition.

Transitions are exciting times. They infuse fresh perspectives, creative rethinking, and renewed energy—all factors that can take a family enterprise to a new level. The transition from the second generation to the third can be a key time for an enterprising family: The family is moving beyond a single household and expanding in size, and the next generation will have values and views shaped by their different experiences. The original purpose that gave birth to the enterprise may have been achieved.

Those coming into their own in the enterprise may not have the same foundation of connection with more distant relatives who helped to ground the enterprise originally. The family legacy may still be valued, but varied interpretations of the mission may drive its newest leaders.

Adopting formal governance structures can help ensure the survival of the family as an economic unit while also preserving relationships. It's valuable to remember that the emphasis in governance is on the family (not the assets). Organizational processes and structures help an ever-increasing membership manage the extraordinary tensions and complexities that are inevitable among a group of people who are both economically and emotionally connected.

At times of key change, such as generational transitions, a family will want to evaluate whether its earlier goals remain priorities—or if they have been achieved. Reasons for joining together can change during a family's evolution, and those reasons need not remain permanent.

A family that shares assets is wise to consider whether its personal and collective goals are still served by staying together when a transition is under way. This may be an ideal time for members to stop and reassess what they hope to accomplish as a family unit. Should we stay together economically? If the goals of the individuals continue to mirror what can typically be accomplished by a family enterprise, then they can confidently move forward. And the governance approach that a family ultimately adopts should be constructed to help it improve the odds of achieving these goals.

Vignette: Forging a New Strategic Direction

A fifth-generation enterprise family had just sold its original business. Its members felt unclear about where to focus their future endeavors, but they knew they wanted to work together in some way. A plan was mapped out that entailed about a year's work. Family members met in generational or branch groupings to discuss vision and mission and to define the shape they thought a new enterprise should take, including operating companies, investments, and/or philanthropy. A kick-off educational seminar was held to update the entire family and bring all the members into the discussion. Working groups were set up to explore initiatives defined at that first seminar. Other meetings followed. It took a full year of teamwork to ultimately redefine the family's core values, vision, and mission, and to shape a new strategic direction that everyone could all agree on.

While some believe there is a general blueprint or governance, governance should also fit the family's vision of its purpose in an elegant way and balance family dynamics. The mission and vision, personal to each family, becomes the compass that steers the course for the enterprise.

Governance defines how the family wishes to organize itself when making joint decisions and encourages participation. It comprises both structures and processes that guide how to achieve its mission and embody its values.

Governance structures give family enterprises the tools to establish order, allow diverse voices to be heard and make informed decisions. From the perspective of setting boundaries, the structures allow family members to participate fully in the enterprise while still retaining their separateness and choice, both of which are critical to sustainability.

Family members have to consider many factors in developing the organizational processes suited to them. What level of organization do they need, based on the family enterprise's complexity and size? How many family members will be involved and in what roles? What should be the criteria for participation? How often should they meet? How will decisions be made?

The structures take many forms. As mentioned earlier, no one system necessarily serves all families or any one family over time. Governance processes should be evaluated periodically to ensure they are meeting the evolving needs of the group. Every major transition in a family is likely to prompt a reexamination of the organizational system in place. And remember that the goal of governance is not to create complexity but instead to enhance the family's ability to manage it.

Once a family has defined its core values, vision and mission, it can then decide on what the entity's members might need to accomplish their mission and vision. These structures, as mentioned previously, will vary depending where on a continuum the family enterprise falls—from owning one business to multiple businesses, to diversifying assets, to selling the family business and investing in the equity and bond markets, or to buying another operating business.

For instance, if the family owns one main business (as opposed to owning a string of diverse businesses), it may decide to form a family council and an advisory board (or a board of directors) to balance the need for family input and provide operational expertise. If the family has mainly liquid investments (in other words, a financial family), it may decide to add an investment committee comprised of family members and independent outsiders, with clearly defined responsibilities and guidelines, to oversee its liquid assets. This committee will set guidelines based on the needs of the family shareholders to deal with risk, asset allocation, return and liquidity.

Irrespective of the assets it holds, families have to decide what is necessary to educate members about such topics as: family dynamics; family holdings; or basic investment education about stocks, bonds and private equity, as well as family member rights and responsibilities related to legal vehicles such as trusts, private trust companies and corporate governance. We delve more deeply into this aspect of human capital development in Chapter 5.

The Shape of Governance: A Thoughtful, Inclusive Process

We believe that everyone who has to live with the decisions of the family enterprise should be involved in some way in making them. For some family enterprises, those voices are heard through trust entities where trustees are legally responsible to give voice to the beneficiary's desires in their decision-making. The net for participation should be cast wide and deep. While this may seem unwieldy, getting everyone on board, including beneficial owners, during the development process can prevent difficulties later on. The first step for most families and their advisors is to define the values and mission for the enterprise. The right governance process is one that enhances the best of the family's dynamics while counterbalancing its most negative aspects.

This development phase of governance can engage a family for anywhere from six to eighteen months. While this may seem like a long time, once completed, the plan will truly reflect the family's values and its needs. Our proprietary tool, The Family Enterprise Sustainability Index, is designed to assist families in identifying where they are on their path to sustainability and where they need to go to achieve it.

Assessment is the first step. Implementing the results and priorities takes time and requires discussion. An informal meeting is not the right setting for the deliberative process that needs to take place over months and emerge from the family's collective wisdom. In the end, however, a family should be able to develop a governance approach that is right for its particular enterprise.

A key element to developing a governance structure involves allowing divergent voices to be heard. Building trust within a family enterprise is crucial. Many challenges result from matters that go undiscussed. The process of working together to resolve such challenges builds trust and produces a sense of shared achievement. But families have different tolerances for communication and transparency; each has to evolve to its own process and its own structure.

Vignette: Aligning Managers and Beneficiaries

Within one broad-based, multigenerational family enterprise, the management of the major holdings had come to be handled by just one of the six family branches. The other five were beneficiaries; none of their members worked in the enterprise, and they felt they had no control. The challenge was to develop a governance structure that allowed one branch to provide management direction and at the same time provide voice and participation of all beneficiaries (represented by their trustees) at the ownership level. Communication and transparency were critical to inspire confidence throughout the family branches. Avenues for frequent and two-way communication were developed and incorporated into the process. This took the form of developing an ownership/shareholder group that met independently to discuss issues that were coming before the group as owners. Representatives of this group also regularly and periodically met with the board of directors of the family's holdings. As the groups met and began to understand the consequences of their current approach to business, the family members active in management and on the business board of directors came to see the importance of sharing a vision for their collective holdings. Otherwise, the beneficiaries would not understand why a short-term cut in distributions might be needed to invest in long-term growth.

As a result of these meetings, an agreement was eventually reached that would allow all the branches in the family to qualify for the three family board seats and to participate in the selection process of independent board members. Over time, these changes served to increase the sense of all the beneficiaries/owners that the managing branch of the family was doing a good job and was paying attention to the needs of the other branch owners. The group also instituted a policy that encouraged internships and employment opportunities to all family members who qualified. Attention to building trust played a huge role in the family enterprise's continued success.

Clearly determining the appropriate level of participation is important. What is decided and by whom is important. For some family enterprises, the family constitution lays out the formal governance process and describes how and when the family assembles and how it does its work. Committees are created; and membership criteria and clear roles and responsibilities for family members are established. Family meetings are defined, as are methods for ensuring that a smaller group of family members is assigned to deal with concerns that come up in between bigger meetings. The relationship between the family, the ownership group and each of the assets that it owns is clearly established so that the board and the family are clear about the nature of their relationships. The constitution also may contain articles that define liquidity and exit options.

Opportunities to opt-out allow family members to have more control over their own destiny and allow them to remain family members in good standing should they decide not to participate in the shared economy. Understanding the conditions and pathways to obtain benefits of ownership, for instance low-interest loans to buy a house or seed a business, is another way in which family members feel more independent and in control. Often, just knowing that staying connected to the family asset pool or to separate is a choice, can deepen the commitment to the family enterprise.

A typical family enterprise works through the implementation of its governance processes over time, modifying them as needed. The ongoing goal is to cultivate an enlightened view of stewardship toward the family wealth and to help the enterprise evolve from one generation to another, for as long as the family desires to do so or perhaps as long as the trusts holding the ownership define the need. Being enlightened ensures a mindset of an owner even though you may have the status of beneficiary.

Participation of family members is usually encouraged from an early age in anticipation of their eventual ownership (either outright or through trusts) of the family holdings. As the family grows in holdings and in membership, ownership is increasingly held in trusts, which have trustees, who in collaboration with the beneficiaries, discuss and decide how to vote on major decisions with regard to ownership.

While beneficiaries do not actually get to vote on matters of the ownership of holdings held in trust, the trustees have a legal obligation and are expected to act on behalf of the best interests of the beneficiaries in making their informed decisions. It is also true that over time, the value of the family group in the ownership decisions also increases but is not where final legal decisions are made. Since all the family is impacted by the decisions made by the trustees and owners-beneficiaries, it is in the best interest of all to take the temperature of the family on a variety of issues related to ownership.

Vignette: Preparing the Next Generation

One family, the Jansens, chose to invite their young people to join the family assembly at age fourteen and become voting members with committee responsibilities at age sixteen. The young people went through an orientation held for new members, and like others, were expected to attend family convocations once or twice each year. Advance preparation and active engagement were expected from all members at the meeting itself.

Another family used a special learning session before full family assembly membership to educate the young people on communication as well as how to read the family business and philanthropy reports, how to ensure confidentiality in accessing the documents, and the care that needed to be taken in discussing family matters via social and other media. The presence of third-party specialists to help in this process eased possible tensions and cross-generational pressures. They were continuously aware of the many ages of, and ways to engage, the next generation.

Governance helps a family stay nimble. When rapid decision-making is needed, a ready process is at hand, and that process is even-handed with clear structures for communication. During difficult economic times or when a major opportunity suddenly emerges, a family forum can be pulled together for a reassessment and rebalancing of expectations. Later, we will discuss the building of resilience as a muscle that permits agility in the enterprise.

Vignette: Transitioning to the Fourth Generation

The Green family had already experienced the transition between the second and third generation and was now anticipating the transition to the fourth generation. In preparation, the family decided to revisit its existing mission, vision and values, and governance structure. Was it working? The family council decided to survey family perception by utilizing the Family Enterprise Sustainability Index and found that, for the most part, the answer was "yes." However, the family also discovered that the next generation was not as connected to each other or the family legacy as previous generations because they were so removed from the original family legacy that began with the business that had been sold 20 years before.

Additionally, the family clan was increasingly more diverse and geographically dispersed. Concern was expressed that the family wealth would be taken for granted and that there might not be the energy, motivation, or sense of connection to grow wealth that existed in the third generation. Would the vision of the second and third generations to be sustainable continue to be realized if they did not actively pull together around a common vision? The family council appointed a task force to work with the education committee to come up with a plan to engage the next genera- tion. At the annual family meeting, with the help of a consultant, a series of sessions were set aside to bring the next generation together and engage these generational members in a planning process that would assess what sustainability would look like in their generation and help them anticipate what they would need to do as future responsible and resilient members and leaders. The second and third generations agreed to be open to changes and recommendations by the rising generation.

Whichever form of governance is implemented, its structure can serve as a valuable laboratory for both younger and elder generations, guiding them on working together and making effective decisions. Young people gain insight into the family values and business and develop leader- ship and management behaviors. Senior family members experience their family relationships on a new plane, playing different roles and step- ping away from the traditional patriarch/ benefactor interactions. Governance strives to organize the family agenda and gain full involvement of individuals in the family enterprise, helping to ensure their march toward sustainability.

Let's revisit the Samson family as they meet the challenges of family governance.

Case Study: The Samson Brothers Family

Family Governance

The Samson family was always receiving emails with invitations to conferences and workshops or with subscription offers to several publications dealing with family business challenges. Most of the family deleted these emails without reading them or after briefly scanning them. But Emmett, partly because of his concern about the growing complexity of the family enterprise and partly due to his tendency to find interest in those kinds of things, mentioned at a working family member meeting a seminar he saw advertised about setting up family offices as a diversification strategy. He said that he would like to attend with a member of the next generation. Dan, his nephew, said that he would really like to go, and they both agreed to report back to the working family after the seminar, thus ensuring that others might also learn.

About two months after they attended, Emmett and Dan excitedly reported to the family what they learned. While family offices were often set up after a liquidity event, many families had started them while they continued to own their companies. They discovered that these family offices were typically housed within the company office space (or as a division of it) with a specific percentage of the company income placed into a fund that the family would invest together. This provided a way for the family to diversify their financial interests and introduced a potential way as well for the family to diversify resources for the family's human capital development.

Around that time, Conrad's youngest child, Peter, was graduating from college with a major in finance. He was extremely interested in obtaining his CFP and CFA so that he could move into the investment arena. While no guarantees had been made to him, clearly this might be a way for not only Peter, but also Dan and Van to expand their interests.

While the family all agreed that a family office was interesting, there seemed to be a bit of disagreement with regard to how to make the decision, the degree of risk they could tolerate, and the way the office would be handled. Family members went back and forth for several meetings with no clarity or resolution of the topic.

The second generation of working family members—Jane, Van, and Dan—decided that if members got together and came up with some ideas, perhaps they would have better success at reaching a decision. They realized that the family had grown larger with multiple interests at work and that the elder generation probably had less need and less risk tolerance for the family office even though agreeing with its usefulness. So, they met twice, two hours each time, and hammered out what they thought might be a good plan that specified how much initial funding should go into the office and a methodology for taking it out of the company in a thoughtful budgetary manner. They suggested that the current CFO, Graham Foster, be asked to make room for the office in his portfolio of

Samson Brothers Family
1996

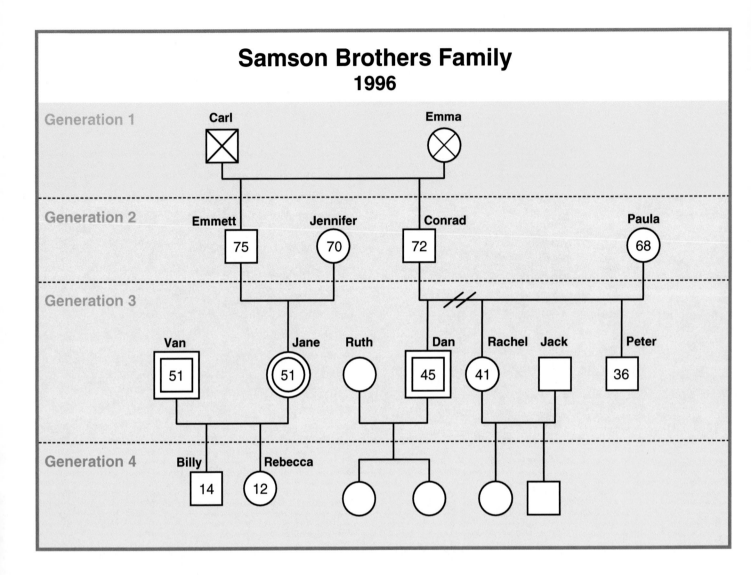

Case Study: The Samson Brothers Family
(Continued)

areas of oversight and that Dan begin working with him on the details of the area. All of the tax, insurance, and other documents would be handled through this area. The family would use this area as a way to invest together, increasing the amount available far beyond what any next-generation individual would be able to accomplish. The bill paying and other services that Conrad and Emmett used would now fall under this area as well.

They suggested that initial funding be in the neighborhood of $1 million, provided, if necessary, by leveraging one of the fully paid-for buildings.

Thereafter, five percent of all profits would go into this area for investing. The three of them decided to run the idea by Graham to get his buy-in before proposing it to the older generation. When they did, Graham became very excited about the prospects, not only for the family as a way to diversify, but also as a potential area of exciting and interesting prospects for him in his position. With that endorsement, the three decided to present their plans to Conrad and Emmett.

At the next meeting of the working family members, Dan, Van, and Jane shared the overall idea for moving forward with the seniors. While it was met with a general positive regard, it was clear that there were many questions yet to be addressed. Emmett and Conrad wanted to know how Graham was going to handle the new area

along with his current work at the company. How/who would make the investments? And how would they be involved as a family in the oversight of such, especially since not all of them understood investments? They wondered how, if the money were coming out of the business, the other nonworking family members could benefit from the investments? They were also unclear about how decisions would be made about the overall balancing of the family's assets.

They all had a sense that they were onto something that could be helpful, but they were concerned that without the appropriate attention to details, it might become another complication rather than a simplification of their holdings.

Figuring out how to structure this vis-à-vis the family and the real estate company would be central. Also, setting up policies to govern and educate everyone would prove helpful in the long run.

While they were considering all of these dilemmas, the family continued to grow; Ruth and Dan were now the parents of twin girls. Peter was getting closer to graduation, and the real estate growth in New York City was increasingly being viewed as a bubble, potentially threatening the family's main source of wealth.

Bob Lanry retired in 1996, sensing that Jane was able to take over the leasing area. Jane and Van's kids were now teenagers demanding more of their parental interest and time.

The Sampson family clearly had reached a stage in their evolution that demanded a different structure for managing their current and future holdings. The structure needed to acknowledge the different needs of the generations in terms of risk and opportunities as well as the different levels of involvement and decision-making needed. Being very thoughtful and deliberative in mapping out the entities and the various constituency groups would be an important first step that later on would lead to less confusion.

Summary
Governance is an essential step in organizing and nurturing the family enterprise so that it can flourish in a constantly evolving economic and social landscape. Establishing a structure and policies for organizing interpersonal dynamics is a stage that families aspiring to sustainability need to take. It provides a framework for resolving problems of trust and connection, formulates explicit and shared agreements about family assets, defines liquidity and offers exit options.

Every family unit typically has an informal, implicit structure for making decisions and policies for working together harmoniously, even those that are not enterprises. But families that share assets and an economy usually require a more formal, explicit structure to reach decisions, consider opportunities, and deal with risks. Governance helps to manage personal dynamics so they can serve as an ally to the enterprise rather than its greatest nemesis.

In the next chapter, we will talk about another key element in sustainability: financial accountability. ■

Financial Accountability and Management

A sign of maturity and adulthood is the ability to be responsible and accountable for one's own financial resources. For enterprise families—in which the amount of financial resources is often significant, complexly held, tied to the family and passed from one generation to another—it can make it challenging for family members, but especially young people, to feel a sense of self and a sense of "ownership" of their finances, especially those held in trusts.

While trusts are legal entities developed to mitigate the estate, tax and credit risks of wealth, they often add another layer of complexity by shifting control and responsibility away from those for whom the trust was established. Thus building self-reliance and responsibility in younger family members must be carefully thought through, since individual accountability will impact joint risk and opportunity.

A family enterprise is a shared economy, in which members rely on each other for the successful management of finances. A powerful heritage unites them—a successful legacy business, a web of connections, and a name with significance and equity in the community. The shared financial accountability for the enterprise can strengthen bonds and at the same time thrust further responsibility and add collective risk onto family members.

The challenges of financial accountability can be daunting. How does the family meet the current capital needs of family members while ensuring that there will be sufficient resources for future generations? How can the family be certain there will be enough equity to go around, without knowing the future? The not-so-distant upending of our economy in 2008-2009 is a stark reminder of how unpredictable our world can be, and the transient nature of money.

Gaining insight into its shared financial responsibilities can help a family shift from being one that owns a business to one that is concerned with return on investments (ROI). Preservation of wealth alone does not lead to sustainability. Older family members say they are kept awake at night by the concern that their offspring will lose family assets through reckless spending or ignorance as to how other actors are handling the assets.

they choose to remain together financially, e family usually has to commit to a policy growing its wealth or agree to settle for e alternative, namely, drawing less and less om the enterprise over the years. The fam-'s shared economy benefits when individual embers see themselves as co-creators, nbracing an entrepreneurial attitude that ks, "How can I contribute to the family's oductivity and development?" Otherwise, e needs of individual members and family xpansion can overwhelm the growth of mily assets.

ocusing on the future is critical. Many differ-it factors need to be considered: spending tes of family members; how current spending tes affect the ability to provide for the next eneration; what assets should be provided r the next generation; options for growing sets; and the "two D's," diversification and vidends. Moreover, providing a means for mily members to exit some or all of the oldings is important—a pruning of the family ee. Lastly, educating younger generations the enterprise, its policies and guiding hilosophy is crucial. Families that embrace uch a perspective are sure to be sustainable.

e Role of the Individual in Oversight
very family needs a plan for regenerating ealth that balances the need for liquidity y shareholders, beneficiaries and owners, gainst what is required for growth. This an works best when it has the backing and formed commitment of every member of e family.

ie best hedge against risk are knowledgeable, otivated family members who view them-elves accountable at the highest level for

managing their shared wealth. This accountabil-ity goes beyond stewardship, to a shared sense of ownership. Family members who can transition from feeling like participant-actors to becoming true owners are likely to exercise greater responsibility in their oversight of the enterprise. Ownership, as opposed to steward-ship, implies a sense of active responsibility.

This sense of responsibility needs to be modeled and encouraged across generations. The oversight role is typically not assigned to outside managers and advisers. No matter how many outside managers a family may have to assist them, those families seeking to be sustainable must retain oversight of their wealth. To do this, they will want to be sure they're getting the information they need, when they need it, and in a form that is understandable and accessible for their use.

Good information, communicated effectively, is crucial. Sometimes reports on financial as-sets can be difficult to interpret; for example, critical issues that need a response may be buried. Especially in a shared family economy, it's important for reports to be tailored to all the members. Documents should be easy for family members at different levels of financial education to scrutinize and understand, high-lighting the vital facts and signaling opportuni-ties or risks. At the same time, they should not be "dumbed down" and should require that most family members have a basic under-standing of financial matters and issues. Over time, we have found that as families alter their financial structures, they may wish to adjust their accompanying communications, trying out different approaches. The following case illustrates this.

Vignette: The Johnson Family

When the Johnson family formed a family limited liability corporation, government regulations required that the next generation be educated and involved. This meant that the young people could no longer play a passive role. Regular meetings were scheduled; and younger members were expected to attend and be actively involved. New reports were generated for their consumption, but the younger family members found themselves unprepared for the volume of information they needed to digest to play a role in the LLC. They were surprised and unsure how to read and interpret the new financial information being thrown at them. In the end, however, the challenge served to engage the next generation in a meaningful learning process and involved the siblings and their parents in a shared project that set the stage for future initiatives in which they would work together.

Family governance systems can help with financial accountability. They formalize communication, assure outreach to all family members and provide a structure for decision-making. These factors build in an expectation of involvement, encouraging personal responsibility and, ultimately, a sense of ownership. When an organization evolves into a fully engaged family enterprise, the payoff is worth it.

Financial Responsibility across Generations

Financial accountability and responsibility are critical to sustainability and to addressing the needs of the various age cohorts in a multigenerational family enterprise. Sustainability has to be a goal that all the generations buy into. On the one hand, sustainability focuses on the future and the youth of the family. On the other, it calls on elder family members to model appropriate values, such as understanding the balance between wants and actual needs.

It's important for families to begin inculcating two concepts in the new and future generation: the notion of need versus want and secondly, the responsibility for oneself and for others. While affluent families do not face the challenge of meeting their most basic needs, such as shelter and enough food to eat, they do face another type of challenge, that of helping their children consciously register they may not really "need" what they "want," and that there is a difference between their lives and those of others in their community and beyond.

It is essential to expose younger family members to the lives of those who are less fortunate so that they can see firsthand that food and shelter are not a given. This may help them understand what "need" really means and that what they feel to be a need is actually a want. In this way, they may learn to distinguish

tween need and want and develop a sense
gratitude for what they have. This in turn can
d to a sense of social responsibility rather
an a sense of expectation or entitlement.
e Chapter 7: Generosity and Gratitude, for
ther discussion of this important issue.)

hen entitlement begins to take root in a
mily enterprise, its effects can be destruc-
e. Knowing the difference between needs
d wants can make a huge difference when
arged with managing personal finances,
dgeting for fixed financial obligations and
ciding on savings versus disposable income
ending. On a larger scale, it can contribute
a recognition of the needs in the world
und them.

ow then does a family go about instilling a
nse of financial responsibility? It does this
ensuring that all members of the family are
t only informed, but also appropriately and
tively engaged in decisions regarding the
ances of the enterprise. Members may
rticipate actively in the governance or
ganizational meetings and structures the
mily has put in place. Younger ones may
afforded opportunities to contribute to

developmentally suitable decision-making
that affects them and future generations
within the enterprise.

Sharing information in a transparent way is
also important. Educational messages get
heard when they are age-appropriate and
meet the interests of the listener. It helps to
have a methodology, a process that specifies
how and when youth of the family gain access
to information (what kind and how much) or
are invited to meetings. The family will want
to factor in the impact of the digital age, too;
today, young people can easily obtain public
information on their family's wealth via the
internet.

However, an untempered imagination often
tends to magnify those assets and make them
appear limitless. In our view, it is better to obtain information directly from family members,
who can dispel misconceptions and provide
context. The question is not how great the
family economic resources are; it is about
how the family wealth is being thought about,
used and managed. Clearly, this is connected
to how the family views its mission (a topic
discussed earlier in Chapter 2).

Vignette: The Dade Family

The Dade family decided that starting at age twelve, each member would take part in a financial
camp, where they could learn about money, budgeting, saving and investing in fun ways.
The learning would continue throughout the year through their ongoing participation in an
investment club, working in the family office with the older generation. This way, when they
turned sixteen and were invited into the family business meetings, they would be better able
to understand the financial discussions going on around them. And if it turned out that they
needed further instruction, they were assigned a mentor (a family member) whose job it was
to assist that learning process. The process moved from an individual sense of accountability
to a collective one.

Vignette: The Fleming Family

The Flemings were fortunate in having built a highly successful family enterprise that was now entering the fourth generation. Their daughters had been relatively uninvolved; they had chosen other careers and life paths. The parents wanted to encourage a sense of shared ownership. They sought their wealth advisers' counsel and brought in outside consultants to help work through some future planning and decisions. The girls' views were explored, and the family considered their interests. Over the next year, the daughters put into the works a plan for a philanthropic initiative, and ultimately, shared administrative control of a newly established family foundation.

On the most basic level, individuals first need to be accountable for their personal finances. From that comes a sense of accountability for handling joint assets. With younger people, it's effective to start with the micro view of their world and then develop that into an appreciation of the family's macro perspective. The more knowledgeable young people become about family assets and the more they see themselves as central to maintaining those assets, the sooner they will appreciate the need for their own accountability and even personal budgeting.

High net-worth families have a convenient economic laboratory to offer their younger members. The youths have an opportunity to see how investments work, to hear how decisions about money are made, and to learn how to take measured risks. This protected environment can accommodate their mistakes and provide them with valuable learning opportunities.

Vignette: The Donahue Family

The grandfather in the Donahue family had been an avid investor his whole life and wanted to help his grandchildren appreciate the excitement of watching assets grow through smart investing. He set aside a pool of money as an investment club. The young people who began meeting with him when they were around ten years old were trained and educated and then given the freedom to choose their own stocks, make purchases and follow the market, modifying their purchases as they chose. Their grandfather served as their coach, providing guidance, questions and facilitation. They learned an enormous amount from both the losses and the profits resulting from their choices.

milies often think that all assets have to be intly owned. Sometimes, it's a case of agreeg on what is going to be jointly owned nd/or on how a family handles what is going be jointly owned. Family financial wealth ay be divided into four buckets: one to bend, a second to save, a third to invest and fourth to give away. An important part of e learning process for any family is how to lance these buckets over the course of a etime. The personal is the start—what it will ke individuals and their family to sustain

themselves. The thinking needs to start with the individual and then move to a discussion among couples or the family branch; all this is a preamble to considering the overall needs of the enterprise for sustainability, in the present and for future generations.

Enterprising families may also want to create policies or structures that promote self-determination and actualization rather than suggesting that reliance on inherited wealth is acceptable.

Vignette: The Tuckerman Family

In the Tuckerman family, the second generation showed scant interest in the family enterprise that had been established and was still being run by the original founding brothers. When the second generation realized that the financial benefits the members were receiving would not be available to their children, they began to get concerned about whether the family resources were being utilized for the maximum benefit of the members. They worried that financial support, such as funds for education and the pursuit of independent business interests that potentially could grow the wealth, would dwindle.

After going back and forth on alternative options, the two generations hit upon an approach that pleased them all: They would establish a family bank. The bank became an avenue for investment, satisfying current members, and also an opportunity for a family loan program that could launch or sustain the commercial interests of future generations. While this approach might appear to decrease current availability of financial resources, the result was to increase the long-term wealth of the family by focusing on human capital development. This reallocation of resources clearly defined the use of assets in the current generation so that the next generations would be able to meet their needs and goals.

Long-Term Management of Finances and Risk

In a very basic way, financial accountability and responsibility represent risk management for families that share assets. Managing personal risk can be far easier than doing so for a large group of people. As a family grows in size, its risk appetite changes and decisions need to be made as to which assets are jointly owned versus those that are owned individually. Different generations have different risk tolerances, and this can make for complicated portfolio management.

Over time, the family may require greater involvement by outside advisers and managers. This can be prompted by major changes in the enterprise, such as the selling of assets, an acquisition, the exiting of family members or a transformation in the business's focus. The use of specialists can add value and help manage risk. But the impact of outside influences on family dynamics needs to be monitored, as it can stunt the accountability of members. The strength of the family enterprise relies on family members' continued sense of ownership responsibility.

Sometimes, trusts are established to protect the assets of younger family members. The appointment of outside trustees can separate individual interests from the family enterprise and remove control from beneficiaries.

Yet trusts can also increase risk for the beneficiaries, as control shifts to the trustees. Trustee relationships can be challenging, and each trustee and beneficiary relationship needs to be considered individually. Sometimes a family member is chosen as the trustee in order to contain decision-making within the family; in such cases it's important to make certain that family dynamics do not get in the way of the kind of objective perspective that an outside expert can bring.

How the role and responsibility of an outside trustee is defined is important. Families striving for sustainability will want to ensure that young people who are the beneficiaries retain responsibility for their wealth and play a central role in decisions regarding its use. In such instances, the trustee is viewed as someone who has the responsibility of working with the beneficiary to achieve financial accountability. In one family, the trustee met regularly with young family members as they were maturing, acting both as a mentor but also defining the nature of their relationship. In another family, the older generation was all too aware of the kind of parental and gatekeeper role that its own trustees had played with members and sought individuals who would take their fiduciary responsibility to the parents' money seriously, alongside their guiding role to the next generation. They asked the trustees to meet yearly with the next generation to review the terms of the trust (after they initially made their children aware of the trusts) and to discuss their children's financial needs and wants.

A family office is another structure frequently adopted by enterprising families as they expand in size and complexity. A family office can be managed by a family member or by an outsider. This executive's role can be that of a financial and/or relationship manager who oversees budgets, manages trusts of family members and helps effect economies of scale while also attending to the differing asset needs of family members. The hiring of an outside manager is likely to be a careful, shared decision within the family. The family will still retain responsibility and oversight and will manage the relationship with the outside manager. The enterprising family needs a clear idea of how accountability happens in their organization.

Vignette: The Johnson Family

A fourth-generation family enterprise was considering whether the time had come to establish a person and place to handle the family business. Investments, insurance, and governance were becoming too significant a part of the workload for the family business operational staff. Once the need for the family office had been clearly defined, a small task force was created to develop the office's scope and a job description for the manager. Because no current family member met the criteria for the job, the family decided to seek out a nonfamily manager. The task force gained family approval, hired a recruiting firm, and interviewed, selected and trained the outside manager.

aving separate advisers is a way individuals an be assured that their interests are being presented within the family enterprise. ven when outside advisers are serving the ntire family, they can present issues related o sustainability. It is inevitable that over time ese advisers will develop more limited ewpoints or will align with some members f the family over others. This is the nature of l relationships. Therefore, family leadership ust be careful to ensure that the best ecisions for all continue to be the priority r the joint enterprise.

ust is another aspect of the dynamic of e family enterprise, as its shared economy epends on the responsibility shown by dividual members. Trust is necessary for stablishing confidence and reliability. But it not something that is a right of inheritance;

it is something that must be earned and built up over time. Making financial responsibility and accountability a core value lays the basis for trust, which is so essential to the sustainability of a family enterprise.

You can again follow the Samson Brothers family as it meets the challenges of family financial management and accountability with the case study on the next page.

Case Study: The Samson Brothers Family

This installment of the Samson family case study examines how the family addressed the need for focused and accountable financial management to serve the future generations' ability to sustain family wealth.

Financial Management and Accountability

The senior Samson generation seemed to have had good estate planning advice and was not worried about its needs financially. Members were interested in creating a joint family foundation since their adviser had suggested that it might be a way to involve their grandchildren in charitable activities, potentially increasing their sense of responsibility for others. Both Emmett and Conrad liked to remind their grandchildren that they were involved in charitable works from the beginning of their careers by providing affordable housing, in addition to housing for the wealthy. They spoke to their children and their children's spouses (or "in-law children," as they tended to call them) about their interest in pursuing this with the grandchildren, and the response had been positive.

Emmett and Conrad were most interested in how subsequent generations were going to maintain their wealth when so many households, those of employees, depended on the family's businesses to provide their income. They were keenly aware of the adage, "shirt sleeves to shirt sleeves in three generations," which suggested that unless the second generation continued to work and add to the wealth of the family enterprise, the family would find itself back to its origins by the third generation, by virtue of increasing membership alone. They recognized that this was a game of numbers and did not want that to be the outcome in their families. They also knew that the next generation was struggling with the same dilemma and wanted to help them.

Conrad grew elderly, however, and Emmett died. While Conrad appeared to still be in good health, he was increasingly frail. Conrad had remarried after divorcing Paula, and his wife, Margaret, about fifteen years his junior, kept him occupied in travel and other leisure activities. He rarely came into the office, and when he did, he would come in, read the mail, talk with each of the kids if they were around, and then leave. On the other hand, during the previous few years, after Emmett had lost his wife, Jennifer, to cancer and seemed a bit lost without her, he grew closer to his children and spent a good deal of time visiting them when he was up north from his home in Palm Beach, Florida. His death felt sudden to his family since he was very involved with them up to the end of his life.

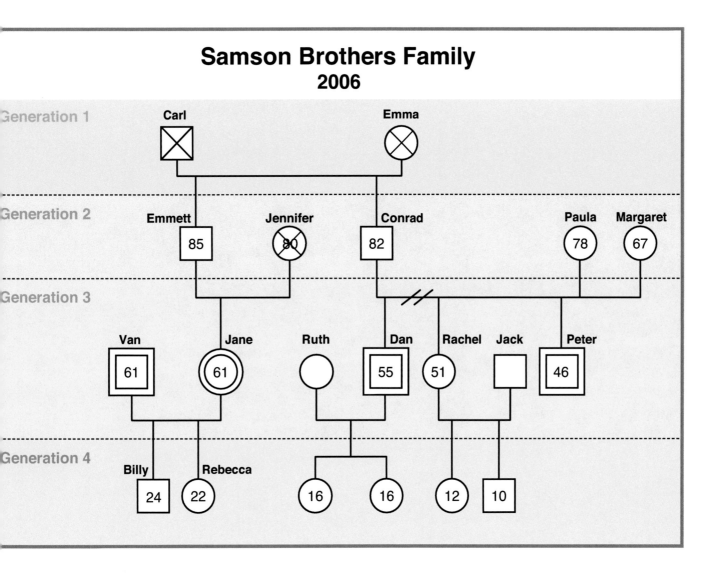

Samson Brothers Family
2006

Generation 1

Generation 2

Generation 3

Generation 4

Case Study: The Samson Brothers Family
(Continued)

With the third generation becoming older and growing in numbers, and the number of family members and owners outside the business increasing, the Samson family began to think about how its wealth created significant new hurdles in terms of its knowledge base. While family members were used to dealing with financial questions related to real estate transactions, they were not as comfortable or as skilled in transactions that were investment-based in the equity or bond markets. They had expanded their diversification efforts and had come to rely on the family office to choose good investment managers, but they felt increasingly outside the loop on these endeavors. Even though transparency was not in question, they did not really understand the details that the family office president, their old company CFO, shared with them about this increasingly significant part of their lives.

Jane, however, had learned to understand the financials from the legal transactions she abided over in her position. Clearly Van, her husband, and Dan, her cousin, were most comfortable, having had finance and investments at the core of their university and post-graduate education. Peter had finally finished his CFA and was getting into the work of the business.

But whenever the family members who worked for company holdings discussed financial data with their siblings and cousins who were not in the businesses, there seemed to be a degree of tension. Perhaps it was because the family outside the business felt insecure with numbers or assumed that those members working in the business had inside information on the investments. An increasing number of questions began to emerge addressing whether someone had "good" intent and whether certain people had the "right" to speak.

Nonfamily professionals began to notice when meeting with their clients in the family that some of them were not able to read the financial statements and couldn't capture a sense of what was happening to their holdings. Peter, now second-in-command of the family office, was beginning to worry about what would happen if this situation were to continue.

More broadly, the family governance was focused on building the family's wealth over time through diversification of assets and liquidity options. But it lacked direction, as there was no specific policy or structure in place for dealing with the family's challenges regarding ROI or risk tolerance. Continuing the discussions solely as family members seemed to encourage the disparity between the insider-versus-outsider mentality, without intending to do so.

Third-generation family members were acutely aware that their own children were being raised in a financial position different from what their own had been. They worried that the value of money had shifted in their families just by virtue of its availability. They were interested in what their father had suggested years ago with regard to teaching the younger generations about money management and accountability. By this time, their children ranged in age from pre-adolescence to college graduates.

he Samson family found itself at a cross-
ads, in part because it failed to address the
uestion of responsibility and accountability
arly on. As a result, trust—the greatest
source that all enterprising families require
 they are to be sustainable—was in short
upply. That said, there were activities and
rojects that were open to them that could
elp to regenerate that trust. We will see
 st what steps the family took to create
pportunities for growing not just assets
ut trust as well.

ummary

esponsibility and accountability for one's
ersonal finances are key milestones in
 ny person's life. But given the significant
nancial resources of enterprising families,
 here resources are complexly held, tied to
 e family, and passed from one generation
  another, reaching that milestone can be
 allenging, especially for younger members.

The effects of entitlement can be destructive
if it takes root in a family enterprise. The
enterprising family's shared economy benefits
when members see themselves as co-
creators, embracing an entrepreneurial
attitude that seeks to contribute to the
family's productivity and development.

The strength of the family enterprise relies
on family members' continued sense of
ownership responsibility. How then does a
family go about instilling a sense of financial
responsibility? It requires education, effort
and creative thinking. The enterprising family
must make certain that family members are
not only informed, but also appropriately
and actively engaged in decisions regarding
the finances of the enterprise.

In the next chapter we will talk about another
key element in sustainability: human capital
and leadership. ■

Human Capital and Leadership Development

*Give a man a fish and you feed
him for a day. Teach a man to fish
and you feed him for a lifetime.*"

—*Chinese Proverb*

Family wealth consists of more than just financial riches. It is the sum total of its well-being and economic capital, including its intellectual, emotional and social capital (known collectively as human capital). For enterprising families who have wedded their financial and emotional worlds, the element of human capital presents risks and opportunities. If families fail to pay diligent attention to the human dimension of the equation, they risk hindering their financial prospects.

In addition to the resources and talents that individual family members possess, human capital also comprises the aggregate of what each family member brings to the whole. In developing human capital, a family strives to ensure that each person has concern for himself or herself, for others in the family, for the generations to come and for the social collective. How a family approaches development of its human capital can determine its long-term sustainability—enabling each generation to address its own needs, while also equipping future generations to provide for themselves. When there's a commitment to developing human capital—where it is viewed as an enduring value among family members with shared assets—the sustainability of the enterprise is virtually assured.

While human capital refers to the value each member brings to the whole family, it is a reminder that it is only as strong as its individual parts. It applies to every family member, whether working in the enterprise or not. For continuity to succeed, it's important that all the members, including those who may have married into the family, feel connected to the enterprise, regardless of the life or career path they choose as they develop and pursue their own dreams.

We refer to the collective talents and capabilities of all family members as the assets in human capital; the emotional, intellectual and social contributions to family capacity. Encouraging individuals to aspire to their full potential benefits them and enhances the shared enterprise. Developing human capital takes different forms in different families: Some have succeeded in building exploratory experiences and learning opportunities to enable personal growth and develop their human capital.

But whatever form human capital development takes, it should respect the personal goals, achievements and career paths of all family members. Strength comes from having everyone on board, understanding the mission and the vision of the family and honoring the gift of ownership that each has been given, while feeling fully capable individually. Families that successfully tap into their human capital resources prosper both economically, through growth of assets, and emotionally, through successful family dynamics and communication.

How do families develop their human capital?
Relationships are the source of energy fueling families. For a family that has bonded its economic and emotional worlds, there is no turning down the heat on relationship attentiveness. If a family wants to increase its economic capital, it must work on the other side of the equation, its human capital—its emotional, social and intellectual assets.

Leadership development is a critical aspect of working with human capital in a family enterprise. If one defines leadership as influencing others irrespective of the position one holds, then every family wants to develop people who can serve as good influencers for the future. Doing so is central for humanity's sustainability.

Over time, different types of leaders will take their place within the family enterprise. Entrusted by their relatives with special authority, they will face the pressure of both managing the assets and relationships of the enterprising family.

Our research on leadership in the family enterprise suggests that skills based solely in the technical and financial aspects of the business may not prepare them sufficiently for the challenges ahead. A family will want to devote considerable attention to selecting and developing future leaders who are able to manage the complex interactions that arise when family members are also business partners.

As the size of both the family and the nature of its wealth and portfolio change over time, it is incumbent on the enterprise to ensure that current and next-generation leaders are equipped to handle the complex tasks at hand. The destiny of the family enterprise will depend on it.

Relationship-based competencies are the most valued ones
"Leaders are made; they are not born," claimed the celebrated football coach Vince Lombardi, and the business world has largely agreed with him over the years. Creating leadership in a family enterprise is particularly challenging: Human capital development has special import for a family enterprise because of the highly charged emotional connections among involved stakeholders. High-profile visibility in the external business world intensifies the pressure on families to effectively develop their next-generation leadership. It can be valuable to look at the experiences of other families when planning development initiatives for your own.

he founders and second-generation leaders
 most family enterprises rose up in a very
fferent world and economy than the one we
'e in today. Industries and jobs seemed
ore permanent. Even the transmission and
sponsibility for the family enterprise was
ss complex than it is today. Given the current
end, however, when industries have shorter
'es and when there is no guarantee that
e jobs of today will be around tomorrow,
aching family members to be resilient,
ialytical and emotionally intelligent becomes
l-important. In addition, those who are
imfortable in culturally divergent situations
e also well-served.

What personal and professional competencies
should a family develop to ensure the longevity
and prosperity of its enterprise? How can a
family measure its effectiveness in developing
its human capital and choosing leaders?

Considering those factors in advance of
major family transitions will allow for orderly
succession planning and smooth change.
Given their mutual accountability and concern for sustaining a legacy to benefit future
generations, family members would be wise
to think about the criteria and competencies
they want to promote in the next generation
of leaders.

Vignette: Addressing the Needs of the Future

For the Winters family, three generations of young family members had begun working in the
family's electrical manufacturing company early on in their careers. As corporate structure became more complex, the younger members were required not only to work outside the business,
but also, upon joining the firm, to serve in many different branches before joining the central
office. These branches were in various locations, including one in a developing nation where the
firm did some of its manufacturing. In addition, the next generation was now required to obtain
some education in corporate and family governance. Learning about their own family history
and patterns as well as their own role in the family dynamics seemed to increase the ability
of young family members to lead with a strong sense of all the stakeholders, including customers,
employees and board members.

New research has shown that relationship-based competencies are among the most important for those who successfully lead family enterprises. In a large and broad-based survey of family enterprises, more than 550 individuals—working family members, nonworking family, peers, subordinates and senior leaders—were queried using a 360-degree assessment process. The process, called the Family Enterprise Leadership System (FELS), was developed by our firm, Relative Solutions. The survey population rated the performance of more than forty next-generation family members working in their family business. Their ratings of the most important competencies showed that factors related to emotional intelligence skills were more important than the organizational, business, or technical competencies traditionally used as leadership measures. A focus on having a narrative for self and family that others can attach to, being a calm, unbiased presence in the face of anxiety and family disagreement, being knowledgeable about the family stakeholders and a demonstrated ability to deal with adversity are consistently viewed as important to leadership, no matter where in the family.

When considering sustainability, a family must ask itself whether it has recognized and created a way to develop these important capabilities in the next generation. These qualities and capabilities are central in preparing the next generation to be responsible members/owners, irrespective of whether or not those members become the leaders of their family.

These recent findings are consistent with emotional intelligence research conducted in the corporate world by Daniel Goleman, Richard Boyatzis and Annie McKee, co-authors of *Primal Leadership: Realizing the Power of Emotional Intelligence*, a book that explains how to use your emotions, not just your thinking, in leading. In 1990, researchers Peter Salovey and John D. Mayer coined the term "EQ" to define this type of competence and serve as a measure of emotional and social intelligence.

In our FELS research among enterprising families, how an individual handled decision-making was regarded as the most important competency. Further, how a leader reached out to other family members, communicated with them, engaged with them in making decisions and delegated functions—these complex decision-making factors were viewed as primary determinants of effectiveness by the FELS research. Careful observance of family legacy, family connections and governance structure were seen to create an environment of mutual respect that fosters sustainability of the family enterprise.

In fact, this makes perfect sense: Human issues can make or break a family that shares assets. Human issues—family issues in particular—add unique complexity to the decision-making in an enterprising family.

ing results-oriented and focused on enter-
ise vision and goals were also highly rated
the research. A leader earned high marks
linking short-term actions with big-picture
mily interests, by adhering to family values
d by understanding his most important
stomers, namely, his fellow family members.
rticipants in an enterprising family have
vested their lives in the enterprise; they
ant to ensure that assets are being managed
accord with their needs and that the equity
the family name is being enhanced.

A number of more traditional leadership
measures surfaced in the research, such as
self-management and conflict management,
but even these were interpreted in the context of a family's sharing of assets. Typical
leadership qualities of emotional intelligence—calm handling of challenges and success in managing personal impulses—were
applauded. Self-interest was obviously not
appreciated when family assets were in play.
However, being aware of and managing the
interests of all stakeholders was important.

Vignette: Developing Leadership Skills

A founder's son, Joseph, had progressed through the ranks and was well on his way to
running the family's furniture distributorship. However, several top salespeople and Joseph's
younger siblings resisted the idea. He was often critical and sometimes became exasperated
in executive meetings, appearing unprofessional and lacking leadership skills. At the same
time, Joseph was frustrated by his father's lack of support and mentoring. Ongoing executive
coaching was put in place for him, as well as a functional organizational structure, complete
with job descriptions, responsibilities and executive development plans. This helped to
stabilize operations and calm discord.

The surfacing of conflict in a family enterprise is something that may be viewed in a positive light. It indicates that family members are engaged, accountable and taking their responsibilities seriously. It also means that negotiation will be core to a family leader's role. Resolving conflicts can be challenging; a family leader needs to balance the interests of the whole against the needs of the individuals, allowing for all voices to be heard and proceeding knowledgeably and sensitively in managing the family dynamics.

One way in which young family members can learn about each other and manage differences is to have opportunities to engage with their generational or age peers in joint activities. Philanthropic endeavors, which also build a collective and spiritual connection to others beyond the family, frequently serve well in this regard. Providing mentoring and guidance to these collective activities strengthens the intergenerational bonds of the family.

Family leaders cannot afford to abuse the status that comes with the role; they must come to understand the boundaries of when to act as owners versus strictly managing the business. It is wise to develop guidelines for all owner-employees because problems can arise at any level in the enterprise from, with, or between family members.

Vignette: Next-Generation Career Development

As the Winters family began to define how it wanted to develop its young members in the business, the family also became clearer about the need to develop all the members of its next generation, whether they served in the business or not. By doing so, everyone would develop an appreciation for the varied roles and responsibilities that go into being a family member with a collective responsibility.

The family council, working with the company board of directors, developed guidelines for relatives seeking employment and strategies for developing the careers of those employed. They viewed the monitoring and mentoring of employed family members to be the responsibility of both the company and the family. Family members wanting to serve long-term in the company would not only have to meet the demands of their positions, but also the requirements that come from being a working family member. These requirements were embodied in a document included in the family constitution called the "Code of Conduct for Working Family Members" and defined the kinds of behaviors expected of family toward other family, and nonfamily, employees.

Vignette: Creating a New Business Structure

The ownership of a manufacturing company, with profits of $20 million, was transferred to three siblings, two sons and a daughter, when their father retired and moved west. The siblings and their spouses made all the decisions. At times, it seemed that very little could be accomplished because there was no forum for decision-making and none of the siblings was a defined leader.

However, the company needed to grow because it now had three families to support. The families needed to define a business plan, a diversification strategy and determine the family leadership. They set up a new business structure, one that compartmentalized the company's sales and marketing, operations, finance and administration and human resources. They decided that within the company, the youngest sibling (a son) would serve as president. This young man was not only extremely competent in finance and administration, but also seemed to have the best sense of how to manage the relationships among his siblings, the future generations and the nonworking family members. Sales rose twenty percent, and diversification could then be considered.

In addition, the siblings worked to clarify the rights and responsibilities of ownership, as well as the differences between ownership and running the company, and established a family council that began developing a program for educating the next generation in relationship-based capabilities. A board of directors was established, sibling conflicts were addressed at both the board and family council level, and the values and needs of the three separate families were discussed. In the end, both family relationships and the shared enterprise were considerably strengthened.

ading a family enterprise is a matter of titude, of conveying and fostering a sense appreciation and gratitude for what others ve made possible and continue to make ssible through their efforts for both the ader and the family. Gratitude obviates ntitlement. And cultivating it in family members is a subtle and worthwhile process.

o one has ever suggested that running a mily enterprise is easy. It can actually be far ore challenging than businesses run by non-

related executives and boards. In the latter case, responsibility and authority are often viewed as more diffuse, and the enterprise is not linked with a family name. Family leaders exist under a microscope, both internally and externally, in how they conduct themselves. Their decisions and actions are scrutinized for, among other things, self-interest and family favoritism.

In addition, their performance is seen as a reflection of the family. External visibility can always be a challenge for family enterprises, particularly if the family is a major presence in its hometown. Family leaders through generations eventually become accustomed to this scrutiny. They learn to manage it carefully because of its potential impact on the enterprise, on family members and on the future generations for whom they hope to provide.

The representative governance model of family enterprises—where the legacy of family and stakeholder ties run deep—puts special pressures on leadership. One approach that serves as a reminder of the "leader within" model for individuals entrusted with family responsibility comes from the Chinese philosopher, Lao Tzu, who said: "A leader is best when people barely know that he exists; when his work is done, they will all say: 'We did this ourselves.'"

In contemporary times, a leader's power can be defined in terms of how that leader exerts influence. The "best" leaders communicate a clear vision for themselves and the organization, understand their stakeholders and manage their perception and influence with them. In this way, leadership is not based solely on defining policy, but on igniting inspiration. Such individuals lead "from within" a family: providing a calm presence, guiding members in the direction the group has determined should be pursued while remaining true to their own principles.

In addition, leaders today have many tools at their disposal that are sometimes seen as adding complexity. For instance, the availability of and access to information can enhance the data available to make strategic and operational decisions, but at the same time the plethora of information makes analysis more difficult. The old saying that things are usually a double-edged sword holds here also.

Human capital: People at their best

When a family's human capital is functioning to its full potential, individuals have an understanding of the shared mission and identify with the values of the enterprise. They are engaged and inspired. And, whether they work in the family enterprise or not, they feel empowered to seek personal fulfillment. Their richness as individuals supports the whole of the enterprise through times of transition, expansion or marketplace change.

The strength derived from human capital doesn't just happen. Like all else in a family enterprise, it thrives with careful nurturing and attention. Each family that shares wealth will find its own way to foster enrichment of its human capital. For some members, participating in family governance can afford opportunities for continued growth and understanding as they take on defined roles and responsibilities. For others, family enterprise activities or shared community initiatives can enhance self-worth while providing insight into family values. A true family commitment to human capital development extends across generations, inspiring individuals to strive for their personal best and contributing to the good of the enterprise.

Vignette: Strengthening Human Capital

A $50 million family partnership was experiencing stagnation. Several attempts to encourage future leaders to initiate new ideas only resulted in lost profits, frustrated managers and disappointed partners. A group of family members began to discuss what steps could be taken to reinvigorate the partnership. One member who worked in the corporate world mentioned the corporate retreat his company had recently held to discuss its strategic direction and what a success that had been. The idea of a retreat struck the others as highly promising. A management retreat focused on strengthening human capital was conducted for senior and middle managers and partners. Here, a strategic planning framework was introduced. Several participants working in different areas of practice had an opportunity to apply the framework to their own practice segments. Action steps resulted from this process, and follow-up on these by family managers brought new energy to the organization.

orporations have formal development plans; families, these tend not to exist. Families at share assets sometimes underestimate ow much mentoring, development, preparation and understanding may be involved. fficult conversations sometimes have to ke place.

eing frank and clear is critical within a family iterprise. While "leading by example" may em like a good approach, it may not be appropriate for young people who are just entering e family enterprise—in fact, they probably ould not try to act like they are the boss.

uman capital development can help guide em to more appropriate roles for them. In the se of the Winters family (presented earlier in e chapter), it was decided that each of the

young family members would have an opportunity to work in another country sometime during their high school or college education. It was important to the family guidelines that they experience what it is like to live in another culture. The Winters family council also designed a program for the next-generation cousins to work with one another in several philanthropic projects to increase their understanding of one another and sense of what it takes to carry out serious financial decisions.

Vignette: Guiding Human Capital Development

Two brothers, who had founded their company twenty-five years before, disagreed about the roles their children, the second-generation cousins, should play in the company. One of the brother's sons had joined the company five years before and wanted an executive promotion. The other brother thought it was too soon to promote him because he showed no signs of executive ability. There were no rules for family participation in the business and no plans for how to include the next generation.

The brothers and their families were helped to explore and define exactly what the business meant to their family. Management, ownership and family relationships were all considered. Over five generations, the family had operated several different sibling-owned companies that were never successfully integrated into the whole. Moving forward, this family established many formal parameters—job descriptions, performance evaluations, participation rules for its next generation—to more explicitly guide development of its human resources and human capital capabilities within the enterprise.

While sustainability of the enterprise needs to be a shared goal among the members of each generation, human capital development is all about the individual. The well-being of one family member can have enormous impact on the others. Their shared legacy bonds them, making it important to everyone that the capability of each person is well developed. The family benefits most when each individual is able to develop to his or her personal best.

Education plays an important role in sustaining family enterprises. The family enterprise can serve as a secure human laboratory providing opportunities to see commerce at work and to learn how to earn, invest and save. Family members can try out different jobs and activities, learn to take risks, make decisions, face challenges and solve problems.

But young people in succeeding generations also need a mechanism for learning business lessons that employment experiences outside the family enterprise can provide. Internships at the college age are a great way for young family members to learn the ropes within the family business or outside at other firms. Mentors within the family can contribute to their learning; senior generations have enormous wisdom to share, if they are available and committed to developing the family's capabilities while still allowing each member to pursue her or his goals and dreams.

It is important not to underestimate the challenges and complications of becoming your own person when you are in a family that shares assets. Family and public expectations may run in a direction that a young person does not wish to follow. Defining your own passion in life and pursuing your own dream is a challenge. Enterprising families will want to provide ways for their younger-generation members to maintain their sense of family connection as they choose to pursue separate paths.

ngoing human capital development, in the ⸱rm of learning, as well as through participa- ⸱on in the family's activities and governance, important for all generations and all levels ithin a family enterprise. Members' shared ⸱nse of legacy and connection benefits from ⸱ntinued renewal and communication. This ⸱n help inform their contribution to gover- ⸱nce within the family organization, and their ⸱lfillment of responsibilities for financial

accountability and stewardship. The active participation of all family members, to whatever degree they choose, enables the enterprise to thrive and to fuel its sustainability over time.

Below you can learn how the Samson Brothers dealt with the fourth dimension of sustaining family wealth—human capital and leadership development—and discover how they ad- dressed the issue of developing talent.

Case Study: The Samson Brothers Family

In this episode of the Sampson Brothers family case study, the third generation began to look ahead toward the leadership of future generations and assess how best to employ the family's human capital.

While considering how to instill financial man- agement and accountability in the next genera- tion, the first cousins (Jane, Van, Dan and Peter) began to focus on what the young people in the family would need to become responsible own- ers, capable of making decisions and stewarding their family wealth. Jane, Van and Dan were clear that this was necessary, whether the young people joined the firm or pursued other careers. They were also clear that they needed to pro- vide a roadmap for the kids, vis-à-vis working in the business, including the rules for entrance and performance expectations.

Since they could not find a good way to decide who should be invited to explore these chal- lenges with them, they decided to extend an

invitation to the children fifteen years old and above, the age at which the family had been inviting the kids to attend family meetings. Much to their surprise, all of the kids expressed interest and offered some dates that might be good for them to get together. The first cousins decided that Peter, the only cousin without children, would act as the third-generation representative to the group. They also thought that since he had no "horse in the race," he would be the most unbiased in his approach to the notion of stewardship and to how family members enter the companies.

Peter facilitated the setting of the first meeting date, arranging for all of the second cousins to get together for about three hours to discuss

Case Study: The Samson Brothers Family
(Continued)

their thoughts and concerns. While each of the cousins expressed varying interest in joining the companies as part of their careers, they were all most interested in learning more about the legacy and direction of the firm. They had varying degrees of understanding what the family business was about but wanted to learn more about basic structures and how the company actually worked. Peter thought that was a great idea and suggested they begin a project of exploring, with their grandparents, both the history and legacy of the early business. They decided to split into teams to do the interviews and to tape them so that they would be available for the family archives.

When Peter reported back to his first cousin and siblings regarding the tone and content of the meeting, they were delighted. Peter's commentary also pointed to some areas to keep their eyes on. Not atypically, Peter noted that each member of the next generation had different expectations with regard to what the business might provide for him or her. He thought it would be important over time to not only give them all a sense of what the business would offer, but also a sense that they should not depend on it for their support. He felt strongly that each of them should be encouraged to pursue a productive life doing something he or she felt passionate about. This led to an interesting discussion among them regarding the dissipation of financial wealth, what sustainability looked like for their family and what it would take for future generations to be able to sustain themselves and eventually their families.

Ruth and Dan said that they had always provided everything for their children and expected them to do the same for their children. Jane and Van had a different viewpoint; while wanting their children to enjoy the finer things that they had learned to enjoy, they felt it was up to their children to figure out how to achieve that goal for themselves. They said that they had begun their estate planning and were leaving a good deal of their assets to a foundation. While providing for their children in trusts, they believed that the money there should be used only for large purchases, such as education, homes and so forth. They had planned this so that the kids, Billy and Rebecca, would view it as their responsibility to develop themselves, their passions and their careers.

When Ruth and Dan asked if they had considered whether the kids' passions might not be remunerative in the fashion that Jane and Van anticipated, Jane and Van responded that they were willing to let that be and see what happened. To Peter, it seemed that the wealth that this generation had become accustomed to, as well as the differences in household values, might become a challenge for the family going forward. He suggested that his sister Rachel's family be included to broaden this as a family-wide initiative.

Along with a program for developing participation and leadership, Peter recommended they also consider discussing the ways in which each of the households viewed their wealth and what they had communicated to the next generation

Case Study: The Samson Brothers Family
(Continued)

regarding it. He thought his cousins needed to discuss among themselves what they thought the next generation should understand about the families' collective holdings and their expected responsibilities: the kinds of educational and experience areas they needed to have in order to understand the businesses and their other holdings; the operations of the businesses; and the trusts that were established for each of them and for the collective group. Peter stressed that he thought the next generation needed some joint decision-making opportunities so that they could learn to work better together.

The cousins offered to work in joint work groups on these subjects with the next generation. Peter said he needed to think about whether such a configuration might impede the next generation from taking responsibility for the work. He believed that doing the work on their own would help in their thinking and allow them to have a dialogue with their parents about their ideas. While he was not trying to parent the younger generation, he was not sure whether he had the capabilities to facilitate the kinds of discussions needed or leadership to do so. He agreed to think about the alternatives, get back to both groups for feedback and then present his ideas about how to move forward.

Summary

he way in which a family approaches the evelopment of its human capital determines s long-term sustainability and viability. Vhere there's a commitment to developing uman capital—where it is viewed as an nduring value among family members with nared assets—the sustainability of the nterprise is virtually assured. Where human apital is merely an afterthought, the future f the family enterprise is in doubt.

Clearly, there are choices to be made with regard to the "how" of developing family members and family leaders. Being thoughtful, systematic and transparent are essential to a good outcome for the family.

In the next chapter we will talk about another key element in sustainability: generosity and gratitude. ■

7

Generosity and Gratitude

*Vhat do generosity and gratitude
ave to do with the sustainability
f the family enterprise, you may
vonder. While it seems appropri-
te to attribute them to people,
is odd to attach generosity and
ratitude to an entity.*

It's been our experience that families who are grateful for what they have and maintain a sense of largesse toward others tend to avoid the potential downside of wealth and offset its burdens. They are able to ground and balance their wealth with a greater sense of self, and are more comfortable with their riches, recognizing the opportunities it brings to them and the community/world around them. In this chapter, we will look at generosity and gratitude and their meaning in the context of family enterprises.

In the Beginning: Defining the Concepts

When we first began exploring family sustainability more than ten years ago, we offered five dimensions, the last of which was titled philanthropy. That was because most of the family enterprises that we had worked with seemed to have a greater sense of purpose in the world and had built many practices to define that purpose.

However, when we offered the five dimensions to our test families and advisers to see if they concurred that they were essential and that the practices within each were essential to sustainability, we were surprised to find that the dimension of philanthropy was viewed differently than the others. For most of the families and advisers, philanthropy was seen as a "value" rather than a true dimension. While we thought of "giving" as an essential contributor to sustainability, their argument was that families could sustain themselves without it. Consequently, we removed the dimension from our online tool but incorporated the notion of philanthropy into some of the other dimensions, such as family legacy and connection and human capital.

The world has changed greatly over the past ten years, and the sense of giving or philanthropy has changed along with it. Multiple trends are driving this shift: the decrease in public funding, the increased amount of wealth worldwide and the growing bifurcation between the high-income cohort and those on the lower rungs. Clearly, the younger generations believe in using philanthropy as a means of enacting social change through personal engagement, direct giving and impact investing. Given these changes, it seems apropos to reconsider the need for a dimension addressing this subject.

But what should it be called? Does a family have to be viewed as philanthropic to be more capable of sustaining itself into the future? How does philanthropy relate to using resources and preserving them for the future at the same time?

It occurred to us that it would be best to examine the underlying concepts of philanthropy and sustainability. We began to think about the relationship between scarcity and abundance and how a worldview based on only one side of the equation would be very different than one based on the other. We also thought about the concept of generosity and what it had to do with the notion of philanthropy and, correspondingly, the role of gratitude in sustaining a family's resources. Are gratitude and generosity related to scarcity and abundance—and if so, then how? Can you have gratitude without generosity or vice versa? Our sense is that it is important to think first about abundance and scarcity and then how generosity and gratitude relate to and interact with them.

Abundance and Scarcity

A person's views on generosity and giving are the products of their upbringing. In my own case, my parents' views were shaped by the twin experiences of growing up in the Great Depression and coming of age during

World War II. Frugality was a virtue to that generation: They had known the effects of scarcity firsthand, and as a result believed that resources were limited and were to be guarded and protected. Although they tried not to let this sense of "self" determine how they interacted with others beyond our family circle, their view was that one took care of one's own first before taking care of the needs of others. My parents were slow to attend to the needs of the community. Of course, these sensibilities and behaviors intensified when my father felt financially vulnerable, such as when his line of work was threatened by the advent of computers.

At the same time that my parents believed resources were scarce, they also held to the idea that their children were to be given whatever they needed to thrive and become responsible adults and contributors to society. They encouraged us to look upon the world as a place of abundance, one filled with opportunities and resources to be utilized. They also supported their children's unique capabilities, without comparing one to another.

In a way, my parents' view of their place in the world was a paradoxical one. For their kids, it meant that we viewed our abundance with a sense of caution. And as Jews who were cognizant of the atrocities visited upon our people during the war, we lived with the underlying sense that everything could be taken from you and you could be left with nothing. Living in a state of growing abundance, yet being prepared for the opposite, became a way of life.

Interestingly, enterprising families share a similar sensibility. They too have faced difficulties in achieving a state of plenitude. Yet they remain concerned about the costs and burdens of wealth and worried whether their children are prepared to deal with scarcity.

hat is the impact of those concerns on
iterprising families? It creates a sense of
otectiveness of resources because they are
en as limited. It sets up a sense of competi-
veness among members to deal with the
nitations, where holding on to what you have
ecomes paramount. Thus, families who do
ot prepare the next generation to dream, to
·ize opportunities and to know that they
in support themselves are more prone to a
arcity model. Preserving wealth becomes
e focus rather than sustaining what you have
id building opportunities. Scarcity is a mind-
·t that may actually result in reducing the
mily's wealth because fewer risks are taken.

owever, families can take action to change
ese mindsets. Stephen Covey in *The 7 Habits
Highly Effective People* suggests a number
' ways to move toward an abundance model,
hich he believes focuses on a sense of op-
ortunity and self-worth. Three of these are
levant to our dimension:

1. Remind yourself that there is more
   than enough;
2. Look for opportunity and acknowledge
   and appreciate all the positives in your
   life; and
3. Give more of what you want.

Gratitude and Generosity
To have gratitude and to be generous, one
must view the world as a place of abundance.
In turn, gratitude and generosity enhance
one's sense of abundance. Focusing on
abundance centers one's operating style on
processes, such as collaboration, coordination
and multiple points of leadership and/or
influence. They are inextricably related and
are central to the sustainability of a family
enterprise.

Gratitude
We define gratitude as an appreciation for
what others have contributed to our own
sense of well-being; it is an acknowledgment
that no one person can do it on their own
and the participation of others has been and
continues to be essential to our accomplishments. It is based on the belief that all people,
especially those close to us, have value and
therefore deserve acknowledgment for their
contributions. Families with this value often
have a variety of practices promoting its
development and expression.

Vignette: The Ahern Family

John Ahern always remembered his father and mother's thankfulness for their small cadre of
employees who served the company through the economic ups and downs of their industry
and locale. While the number of employees had grown, John and his own family continued to
celebrate and acknowledge their participation in events, scholarships, bonuses and community
giving. The family was always grateful for their success and did not see it as their achievement
alone but the result of the involvement of their workers.

The Aherns passed down this belief in gratitude and ways and ways to practice it by sharing stories, written and verbal, which noted that their achievements were possible only through the assistance and participation of others. There was a sense that their success did not entitle them to special treatment but rather gave them a special responsibility to balance the equation. Their children never felt defined by what they had but rather by what they did vis-à-vis others. There was a strong sense of community or communal responsibility.

Families like the Aherns tend to extend this "social compact" to a larger and diverse global community. Frequently, their offspring are provided with opportunities to participate in experiences where involvement does not depend on the ability to pay. In this way, they are more assured of having experiences that are inclusive of others from different cultures and socioeconomic backgrounds. At the same time, the next generation is expected to be able to take care of themselves in the world in terms of daily living.

In contrast, the Grants who are also very accomplished as a family, had a different culture.

Vignette: A Third-Generation Owner

TJ Grant was a third-generation owner of the family real estate development firm. Both his father and grandfather had been very successful in the small city where TJ grew up. He always heard stories about how both of these men were very strong, self-made people who relied on no one for their success or failures. They very much believed that closing a deal left nothing on the table and made one a winner. They were known by the tradespeople in the community as hard bargainers for services. Their employees admired them but never felt appreciated or rewarded for their own accomplishments. Personally, TJ felt the same way—his experience was never appreciated for who he was or his contributions to the company's success.

ratitude embraces a spiritual sense of thank-
ulness for what one has and what one has
een lucky enough to achieve. By "lucky," we
ean that what a person achieves is never
ue completely to his or her own actions and
forts but is the outcome of forces that we
o not totally control.

Those people who feel gratitude recognize that what they may have is not theirs as an entitlement. It is not a given, nor a right— it is partially earned and partially due to the participation of other people or forces.

Vignette: Promoting a Sense of Gratitude

Gloria Green was the fourth-generation member of a large family enterprise on her mother's side of the family and heir to a fifth-generation fortune, which resulted from the sale of her father's family's manufacturing company. From the family stories she heard early on, she had always been struck by the how grateful everyone on both sides of her family were for their "good fortune." While the family believed that they had worked hard to achieve success in their companies and other endeavors, they were also aware that the timing of their sales, and the "luck of the Irish" as they called it, had always been instrumental in their success. Yet she also noted that family members always accepted responsibility for those decisions or circumstances that did not go right; they were able to look systemically at what else outside of their direct control might have affected the decisions. She began to keep track of those family practices or behaviors which promoted this sense of gratitude.

Generosity

Like its sister concept, generosity has to do with relationships, not just self. It is the willingness to share with and give to others that enriches one's life experiences and leads to growth. It speaks to a sense of abundance and largesse, and the willingness to make that a part of one's interactions with others. Without a sense of plenitude, individuals or families keep personal possessions and other items of value "close to the chest," guarding it as one would a scarce resource.

Going through life with a sense that you are part of a larger world with individuals who have more or less than you and your family is the essence of the social compact. When all people are doing well, we are all doing well, and the balancing of resources increases the functioning of everyone! To be generous acknowledges this social compact and seeks to balance the resources a bit more.

Creating resources for oneself or one's family, whether financial or not, is a positive thing. But doing so without a sense of purpose or meaning can often, in our experience, leave people feeling ungrounded, purposeless and empty. A sense of worth is not defined by money, but rather by what you do with it. It is important to create your own success, but it is also important to think beyond yourself, in what you do with it, that is the purpose of your success.

Vignette: Growing Your Own Abundance

While he was growing up, Gregory noted that his family spent a good deal of time in "doing service" for others, as they called it. At first, he was not sure where the idea to do so came from or what it really meant to his family or him. Then his family began including him in the process of thinking about the purpose of their giving—why do we give? What do we want to achieve? He began to grasp that it was not the philanthropy that was the focus (although that was significant)—but the sense that abundance should be shared with others. And in doing so, you grow your own abundance, if not directly or materially, then by the way you experienced yourself.

eflecting on the current state of things, if the ;ing generation is an indication of how suc-·ssful the previous generation has been in ising them to have a sense of responsibility ward others (as well as oneself), then one iuld say that they have been successful. The illennials as a group think deeply about their ipact and/or footprint on the world. Theirs is been a global generation. They have trav-ed more than other generations and have een educated together with people from di-·rse cultures. Their parents' travel, the first uly recreational travel, was more attuned to eing the sights and cultural highlights of her countries and cultures. The rising gener-ion has traveled to experience and immerse emselves in different cultures. All genera-ins have followed suit with many financially iccessful families taking family adventure ips to new cultures.

lichael Moody and Sharna Goldseker have ost dramatically captured the thinking of the ounger generations in the book, *Generation npact: How Next Gen Donors are Revolutioniz-g Giving*. While the group interviewed for iis study were clearly offspring of financially iccessful families, the idea of wanting to eate a sense of balance in the world and to ven the playing field" for all seems to be focus for most of the next generation of ealth. Some might view this as a byproduct f feeling uncomfortable or burdened by their iearned wealth. But even if that is so, the itcome has led to an increased and early icus on improving the world, on using their esources for things beyond self and for the ood of all people. Using their resources for npact is important to millennials. They elieve in living their values: consistency in hat you believe and what you do is a central

tenet of this generational cohort. There is an effort to change policies that impact our own culture negatively. Some of these examples are the "Me Too" movement and the anti-human trafficking effort. These movements are not simply driven by one social class but rather by all.

So how do gratitude and generosity impact sustainability? It's easy for most of us to see how working on or improving the internal aspects of one's family will lead to the ability of the family to evolve with each generation. Often, this is focused on wealth generation and increasing the capacity of the next generation in leadership and human capital. We would argue that working together on giving also increases a family's sense of connectedness and provides other avenues for developing human capital and legacy.

However, the ability to make a connection between increasing family enterprise sustain-ability and focusing on characteristics that are essentially externally directed towards the larger community is a leap for people. We suspect that may be why when we earlier offered this dimension as "philanthropy" it was rejected and not seen as essential. However, it has become clearer in recent years that in order for us all to survive on this planet, we must think about others and about how we use the resources around us and for what purposes. To the degree that everyone does better, we all do better, and the planet and its people do better. Now almost ten years after the initial development of our concept of family enter-prise sustainability, the world has gained much greater clarity on the need for sustainability and what actions will increase the likelihood of achieving it environmentally and culturally.

Case Study: The Samson Brothers Family

The origins of the Samson family's philanthropic efforts can be traced to Emmett's wife and Conrad's wives, Jennifer and Paula, who initiated the family's charitable giving as Emmett and Conrad's business grew and became successful. From the very beginning, Paula and Jennifer were determined to involve their children, Jane, Dan, Rachel, and Peter, in their effort. Early on, the second generation gave of their time, working at community soup kitchens and homeless shelters, and providing food for needy families.

Jane, Dan, Peter, and Rachel began to be involved in much broader political changes, organizing and campaigning statewide for housing for the homeless.

As an entrepreneurial real estate family, the issue of homelessness became the Samson family's focus. They started to get interested in looking at microeconomics, using their own money to set up loan programs for women and families so that they could begin to develop their own businesses and become entrepreneurial.

The six children in the fourth generation began traveling with their families to different parts of the world. Oftentimes, rather than just traveling in a luxurious manner, the Samson family decided to involve themselves in different kinds of charities so that they could really see the places they visited and make good use of some of their time there.

When they went to Africa, they worked with local women who were developing organizations and projects to be able to support their families. They did the same when they went to Guatemala and other Latin American countries to involve themselves in programs that those organizations were doing.

After the sale of part of the family company, the Samsons decided to set aside a larger portion of the proceeds from the sale towards philanthropy and to set up a cross-generational committee to explore how to best utilize the proceeds. The committee consisted of a minimum of two members from the third generation and three members from the fourth generation who were sixteen years or older.

At the committee's first meeting, they involved all the fourth-generation cousins in a local project, so that they would not only have an opportunity to give of their time and energy but would also learn how to work together as a team. More importantly, they had fun and enjoyed the experience.

They continued to meet as a group for a few years, broadening their scope and discovering where their passions lay before presenting the broader family with a plan on the direction of the family's philanthropic efforts going forward. They explained their thinking to everyone, making certain that there remained a focus on the local community, where the family enterprise had begun, but utilizing their family wealth for a larger, more global, initiative.

Samson Brothers Family
2010

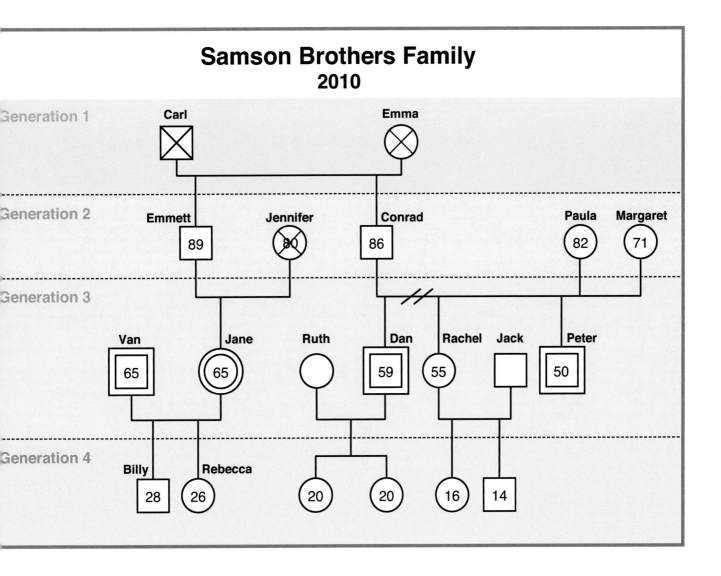

Generation 1

Carl

Emma

Generation 2

Emmett 89

Jennifer 80

Conrad 86

Paula 82

Margaret 71

Generation 3

Van 65

Jane 65

Ruth

Dan 59

Rachel 55

Jack

Peter 50

Generation 4

Billy 28

Rebecca 26

20

20

16

14

Summary

Families who have a sense of gratitude for their good fortune and are able to share that fortune with the world and community around them tend to avoid the pitfalls of wealth. They are more grounded and balanced and generally more comfortable with their wealth. Rather than seeing their riches as a burden, they see the opportunities it affords to make a difference in the world. Having worked with families for decades, we believe that giving is an essential element to the sustainability of the family enterprise: A family's ability to work together on giving increases the bonds between its members and serves in developing human capital and legacy. ■

Resilience

"The longer the legacy and the longer the history and the deeper the habits, the harder it is to change."

—Patty McCord, May 29, 2018

Legacy, history, habit, change: These are issues that face every living entity; from the lone individual to the multigenerational family; from small local businesses to complex multi-national corporations. In the quotation above, Patty McCord, a consultant to some of the biggest companies in the United States, was discussing the challenges large corporations face in building a culture of resilience. But her comments are equally applicable to families where there are long histories and deep connections—and thus perhaps entrenched patterns. If corporations have difficulty shaking off the habits and approaches that shaped them in the past, then how much more difficult is it for a family enterprise to change, given long term relationships, old patterns of behavior and a desire to promote legacy? Add in the wish to maintain the status quo—and the challenges become even greater.

Because of the long-term shared emotional history and tight boundaries that are chief characteristics of family enterprises, the combination of the two factors makes it difficult for families to remain open to change and to be resilient. At the same time, another essential attribute of family enterprises has always been the need to maintain a legacy—a need that often collides with the demand to change.

hat is why it is so important to frame and con-der the idea of legacy differently than the way is typically approached. Families often tend o think about the notion of legacy in terms of dhering to the past and time-honored ways f doing things, whether that is operating a usiness or behaving well towards one another ithin the family. But legacy is actually a living ing, rather than something fixed in stone: is something that each generation builds on, anges and makes use of. It's important to eparate "dead skin"—the ingrained patterns, e habits, the knee-jerk tendencies—from e living tissue that is necessary for growth, stainability and resilience.

ow more than ever before, family enter-rises are faced with the need to contend ith rapid and constant change. The need to aintain what was before, that is, their sense f legacy, may make the challenge of dealing ith change greater. The idea of keeping a gacy has the potential risk of promoting closed system that is cut off from societal ifts and new ideas from beyond their elatively small circle of friends and connec-ons. This closing off from the changes taking ace around them may have an opposite ffect to the one intended; rather than reserving the legacy, it puts it into jeopardy. /ithout engaging in the world fully, families o not have the opportunity to be aware f the changes that have potential impact n their legacy and thus sustainability. In ddition, over time, families who do not ngage with change find themselves becoming ss resilient and less able to handle change. deed, a recently completed study of enter-rising families (Jaffe, 2018) found that families at have been around for one hundred years ere more enduring and tend to demonstrate e ability to be responsive to the need to ange. Developing resilience demands an penness to change and a developed capacity

or methodology to deal with it. Since this capa-bility seems to enhance sustainability, let us take a look at what it means and what it does.

What is resilience? It is the capacity of any system, organization or individual to absorb disturbances, positive or negative, without impacting the nature of the entity and its sustainability. The ability to continue perform-ing while being impacted is essential to the continuity of any organization—perhaps not in the same way or with the same purpose, but continuity all the same. Without it, the system will be hampered. Family enterprises must develop the ability to anticipate the changing shape of risks and opportunities before damage occurs. It is hard, yet absolutely necessary, for family enterprises to be able to change in the current business/social environment.

Resilience is fundamental to the notion of agility. To be agile is to be able to operate quickly and flexibly, yet decisively: to capitalize on the benefits or opportunities of change while avoiding their negative consequences. Resilience rests on the ideas of what it takes to be sustainable and what it means to success-fully meet disturbances along the way.

We believe that resilience is a better measure of success or failure than the achievement of any particular goal. It is the ability to intrepidly jour-ney in one direction and quickly readjust when presented with new data. The key or essence of resilience is that it does not change the core of the family enterprise—that core remains the same. Families need to define their values, mis-sion and develop their systems for the long haul—this will serve them well in the managing of shifts. Instead, what happens is that you have a way or a method to meet changes in the envi-ronment and in the landscape. So, what are the characteristics of resilience—and how can these elements be developed?

There are seven characteristics of resilient people and systems:

1. Optimism;
2. Belief in one's self and having others believe in you;
3. Living to learn;
4. Being curious and caring;
5. Staying in good humor and health;
6. Being realistic; and
7. Taking a positive view of stress and change.

Optimism

A view of the world as a positive and abundant place goes a long way toward creating a sense that one is not only capable of dealing with challenges—but also takes pleasure in having the opportunity to meet those challenges. This sense of positivity influences the ability to feel generosity towards others and gratitude for what one has. Studies on positive thinking have found that people who view the glass as half-full rather than half-empty feel more capable of filling it the rest of the way.

Belief in one's self

Believing in yourself and in your capacity to deal with both stress and opportunity are essential to feeling that you can deal with any obstacles along the journey. That sense of self-confidence, however, needs nurturing and positive reinforcement. For young people especially, knowing that there's another person who has faith in their capacities can make the difference in being able to focus and move forward. If you ask any leader, they will tell you about the one person who truly "believed" in them—knew that they could reach a goal even when they themselves did not possess such assuredness.

Belief in one's self and in one's capacity comes through experience, not through accolades or rewards. It is not something you get from someone saying: "Good job." Instead, it comes from truly feeling that one has done a good job; that you had a goal and tried your hardest to reach it. It is the process and the effort of trying, not necessarily the achievement of a goal, that matters most. Saying someone did a good job when in reality they did not can often lead to a false sense of competence.

In our work with the Ahern family, several of the young family members shared with us that at times Jean demonstrated more faith in them than they had in themselves—and that usually was when they felt least "worthy." Jean understood that the goal was to trust oneself and one's capabilities—and that collaboration rather than competition contributes most to one's sense of competence.

Vignette: The Ahern Family

Jean, the second-generation matriarch of the Ahern clan, would engage each year with the youngest generation, seven years old and above, to discuss the projects they were working on and what they wanted to see as an outcome. She would spend many hours working with them individually and collectively to help them develop a plan to reach their goal and alternative strategies. Offering her support of their efforts and asking about what they were learning was a central part of her time with them. When meeting with them collectively, she encouraged them to be collaborative and supportive of one another.

ving to learn

dividuals who grow up in families that encour-
e learning are best able to anticipate and
eet the demands of change. If you view every
y as an opportunity to learn and explore,

there can be no experience—no matter how
far off the defined path—that is not a chance
to develop the self. It is in the process of
dealing with the risks or opportunities that
provides for growth.

Vignette: The Grey Family

In the Grey family, the parents, Jan and Michael, were people who approached life with gusto.
They frequently volunteered for new and different experiences in their community. They
acted as their own "chief learning officers," making sure that they had a new thing to focus on
for their own education. They not only provided their three children with opportunities but
also most importantly shared their own experiences—their struggles as well as their successes.
As a consequence of their effort, their children entered adulthood with many experiences in
learning that left them craving for more.

ing curious and caring

ving to learn involves curiosity, openness
d caring. Being curious or open means being
cessible to information and knowledge, while
ring entails being giving toward others.

ıe James family was clearly one that encour-
ed engagement in the world and with people.
the process, they taught their younger family
embers to care about those around them.
is curiosity about others expressed itself in
interest in other cultures.

A postscript or prelude to this curiosity about
others may be a curiosity about the self. Our
view is that the process is a circular one, with
each aspect of the curiosity enhancing the
other. However, its essence springs from the
capacity of the older generations for being
curious about themselves and those around
them. The James family had a happy tendency
not to jump to conclusions but rather to seek
out answers and insights.

Vignette: The James Family

The James family was known among its neighbors and colleagues for the dinner parties and
other gatherings it hosted for friends and associates. "It was not the food, which was of course
great, that drew us all to the parties," said a close friend of Mark's (the senior James), "but
rather the interesting group of people and the interest that the family members took in those
who came to join them." The family members, including the youngest members, were always
welcoming and full of questions, which expressed their curiosity in the people attending as
well as the world around them. You felt cared for by their interest.

Being in good humor and health

The body—physically and emotionally—must be in good order to meet change and opportunity with fortitude. It is a challenge to manage the energy and bandwidth necessary to deal with risk and opportunity. Thus, both good humor and health are essential attributes of resilience. Being in good health allows one to be resourceful. And good humor is equally important, promoting positivity and revealing the lighter side of challenges that might otherwise seem insurmountable.

Vignette: The Apple Family

The Apple family was always full of good cheer. They believed in taking care of themselves physically and combined that characteristic with their love of the outdoors. They always entered situations in good spirits and were able to laugh at themselves as they moved through their lives. They often had family nights in which the children were encouraged to put on funny skits and to see the humor in the world and to poke fun at themselves and their family. In later adulthood, when working with his brother Tom, Ricky was asked what he thought the underlying characteristics were of their great working relationship. Ricky mentioned the family's focus on positivity and noted that he and Tom always assumed that the other had their best interests at heart, that they assumed each other's positive intent.

As we have seen, families that invest in the health of their family members increase the family's resources immensely. Further, as families grow and fewer members tend to be directly involved in the family enterprise, the family connection is increased by the connections made in focusing on developing people. Being able to laugh together and to see the funny side of situations is a quality that can be promoted in family activities and communications.

Laughter relieves tension, freeing up the mind to see new pathways and connections. At the same time, it is important not to confuse fun with laughing at another person: Poking fun at something suggests that there is another way to view it (as opposed to making fun of something). And being able to view all aspects of something permits one to begin to think through a pathway that might not be so readily foreseeable.

Thus, having a sense of humor can be a good barometer of how you see yourself and others. It introduces the ability to be playful in one's perspective of self and vis-à-vis others. It connects us to our humanity and is seriously (!) important to our happiness. When someone laughs, it introduces laughter and possibilities to a situation. According the late psychoanalyst Viktor Frankl, who survived the Auschwitz and Theresienstadt concentration camps during World War II, humor reflects our humanness, the ability to detach and look at ourselves, other people and situations from a distance. It introduces a different sense of perspective.

Vignette: Using Laughter to Dissipate Tension

John frequently got into business disagreements with his brother, Raymond. When they would differ on a subject, Raymond would tend to get accusatory of John, suggesting his inability to think clearly or plan was at the root of whatever issue they were having at the time. John would immediately become defensive and justify what he believed or had done, and then Raymond would say, "You have always done that." After one of these situations, John got to thinking and then chuckling to himself, since they reminded him of what would happen when they would play basketball. John would not think ahead (he acknowledged), Raymond would chastise him and, then either John would jump into action or Raymond would, poking fun at him the whole time.

John continued to keep this playful basketball analogy in his mind, using it whenever disagreements arose: acting like he was throwing a ball into a net or passing to his brother. Both would laugh, and the tension between them would dissipate.

using Realistic

realistic sensibility involves understanding hat can be achieved or expected on a actical level. Individuals who think analyti- lly and realistically are able to apply that opportunities and risks. They are able to easure the risk in a situation, weighing the nefits versus the risks to determine the lds of success. They do not tend to overesti- ate their own abilities nor underestimate the hurdle before them. While some may attribute this characteristic to genetics, it is a skill that can be taught to children.[1]

It requires that parents and other adults provide the next generation with the opportunity to assess a situation or a problem and plan a strategy for mastery. With the process of assessment comes the ability to look realistically at what is in front of you and at yourself.

Vignette: Setting Realistic Expectations

Cory was a young middle-school student who came from a very affluent family. While his family had surmounted great odds to attain their current level of success, Cory had not had much experience with adversity. Whenever he had trouble in grade school, such as with completing his work or behaving in class, his teachers and the principal would not be surprised to find his father or mother or both at the school within a day or at times, hours, after a report was sent home. Often, his parents would berate and blame the teachers or the school for not understanding Cory, who was intense and hyperactive. After numerous occurrences, the school decided that this was not helping anyone, least of all Cory, who accepted no responsibility for his behavior and was less and less able to make adequate judgements about the nature of tasks.

Ms. Abernathy, his history teacher, suggested that his parents help Cory to map out assignments and his approach to it. She thought it might also be helpful for them to assist him in estimating the bandwidth he had to do the task in terms of other assignments and his degree of tiredness. They were to have him agree to a plan and hold him to complete it; and if he thought it was getting to be a problem, he should seek out the assistance of his teacher. It would not be acceptable for him to not do the assignment, complain to them that it was overwhelming and have them intervene with the teachers/school.

While it took time for this strategy to work, Cory's ability to be more realistic in his approach to his assignments became noticeable. And both Cory and his parents began to have more realistic expectations of him and his work.

ome people may think that being realistic is e opposite of the idea of pursuing one's eams or passions. In our experience, a dose realism in one's approach to the world helps e pursue one's dream and evaluate the verac-v of them. Developing realism or being realis-: means that one applies critical or analytic inking to ideas and situations. As we will see, aluating situations with a clear measure of pectation and risk is important for managing ess; the ability to deal with stress increases e opportunities to apply such thinking.

Positive View of Change and Stress

'hen I first started out as a psychologist and mily therapist, stress was viewed as a great il, and there were various professional scales measure a client's stress factors so as to :termine the patient's susceptibility to illness. was believed that too much stress in a ort time frame would negatively impact the ysical and/or mental health of the person periencing it.

ur modern-day understanding of stress and e role it plays in life has since evolved. In and itself, stress is neither a positive or negative. ther, it is the body's way of responding to any nd of demand, which it does by releasing emicals into the bloodstream, increasing the art rate and constricting the blood vessels protect the vital organs.

ecent research suggests that it is not the nount of stress that makes the difference in e's health, but the perception of that stress lcGonegal). Those individuals who viewed ess as positive and growth producing did not iffer significant side effects. Those people ho believed stress to be harmful actually iffered higher mortality rates.[2]

People who have experienced abnormally large amounts of stress seem to have a different perception of it than those people who have experienced it less frequently. The opportunity to deal with stressful change gives one more opportunities to learn how to deal with the effects. Such people tend to view stress in a positive light. The better one becomes at dealing with the demands of stress, the greater the ability one will have to use critical thinking in a demanding, change-oriented situation.

Critical thinking is also important in developing the capabilities of young family members and potential leaders. It means that a person can entertain various viewpoints, collect and analyze data from a variety of sources and places and do so in a systematic manner. It is a self-guided process that encourages one to think through options in decision-making. It is an attempt to reason at the highest level of quality in a fair-minded manner. It is also a circular process, because the more you can think critically, the more able you are to manage the demands in typical and atypical situations.

Circularity and Resilience: Developing Resilient Families

Sustainability defines the structure for moving forward if a family enterprise chooses to do so. As seen, resilience provides the method for making right and left turns on the pathway toward sustainability—directional curves that do not disrupt the core of the organization but allow for it to make shifts over time. Sustainable organizations of any kind need the ability to do this. Being resilient increases the ability to be sustainable. And, clearly, all of the characteristics discussed above are inter-dependent. For example, the capacity to deal with anxiety improves the ability to self-guide, to think critically. It is important to keep in mind that resilience is not something one is born with—it is something one develops. It's important to keep this interconnectedness in mind as one thinks about developing resilience, as change in one part of the dynamic process changes the other parts.

How do we develop resilience?

We believe there are several kinds of opportunities that enhance all the interdependent elements of resilience. To develop a more systematic approach to resilience, it's best to view it as a muscle that grows stronger the more it is exercised. Mindfully devoting time, energy and emotion helps develop the muscle. There are a variety of experiences that help. First, basic experiences that promote self-confidence are important. Secondly, it helps to develop an understanding that making mistakes and failures are part of the path towards resilience. Lastly, having the chance to think through situations/options, to strategize and to problem solve is an important skill that one has to eventually learn to do on one's own.

Actively planning these kinds of experiences are not central to the lives of most families. There are frequently many "naturally occurring events" that present themselves. However, these kinds of experiences are not always central to or naturally occurring while growing up in prosperous, enterprising families. And, perhaps, because resources are so plentiful, family members also tend not to be systematic in providing opportunities for enhancing resilience. In our experience, developing resilience requires that families become mindful about embedding this way of operating into their lives. Thinking about resilience-enhancing opportunities across all of the dimensions of sustainability can provide a framework for planning. Let's review some of the opportunities that exist within each of the five dimensions.

Family Legacy and Connection

Providing a young person with a sense of values and mission gives a core sense of what one stands for. The ability to be resilient increases if one has a sense of value and purpose that one lives by. It permits a family member to keep focus even as adjustments are made. Thus, involving younger family members in the process of a values clarification is helpful. While values provide one leg of stability, the other is offered by a deep sense of family connection, of knowing that there are people who care for and look out for you—that are imbedded in your life—that are guardrails as you explore boundaries outside the family. These are basic opportunities that this dimension provides.

Governance

The dimension of governance provides the opportunity for a family to think systematically about how decisions can be made and to evaluate what works or might work, given their family's dynamics. Our experience suggests that this is a time when families can take a look at their purpose and learn to reevaluate their actions as individuals and family members vis-à-vis their sense of purpose. Setting up structures and policies that permit the family to make decisions more thoughtfully will aid the focus on critical thinking.

Financial Accountability and Management

This dimension reflects the family's efforts to develop and maintain a sense of oversight of their financial holdings; their ownership of assets. In this regard, knowing the questions to ask and the guidelines to establish requires the ability to perform due diligence; to think critically. Developing competence and capacity in these areas is an outgrowth of managing increasingly complex financial questions as well as one's own financial life. Giving a young person increasing amounts of money to manage in their own life is one way that families offer resilience-based training. Being given a certain amount of money per week, month or year to budget and spend provides some opportunity to learn about and feel increasing competence around money matters. This is especially true when some roadblocks are provided along the way.

Families can begin to get young people ready for this responsibility by talking with youngsters about how spending decisions and allocating money and resources are made by the family. While they may not be able to participate in the process, they begin to learn how others think about the situation and the successes and mistakes the older family members experience as they have moved through their lives.

Leadership

When families approach the development of leadership, resilience is a central quality to encourage. Without this quality, next-generation family members will be unable to deal with the ups and downs of family enterprise ownership. They need to be able to identify when change is imminent and demands a deviation from the path forward. They need to have confidence in their ability to manage the change and provide a clear path forward that others can trust and follow. Having had experiences that demand a test of their capabilities to organize and lead projects, beginning with small ones, like an activity for the family reunion, to managing an investment project for the family office, offer increasingly complex leadership tasks that allow them to develop the resilience muscle.

Generosity and Gratitude

Being able to be generous toward others and show gratitude demonstrates the ability to go beyond self and be involved with others. For young family members, it means seeing yourself in the context of your family as well as your family and yourself in the context of a broader world. It recognizes connection to others responsibly. For most families, providing young people with experiences that are leveling—that demonstrate that people are more alike than different—begins early on by providing the opportunity to participate in activities with all kinds of diverse people. Acknowledging abundance and being generous with others begins in family activities that devote time to others. Participating in activities that demonstrate to others how grateful one is for their assistance is another way to go beyond self. This focus on boundaries and context provides the tableau for opportunities to develop, increasing a capability and sense of competence in dealing with the world around the family. It becomes hard to be insular when the focus is outward.

Clearly, having a general attitude across the board that focuses on the responsibility to provide resilience exercises and a thoughtful plan to do so is essential in resilience-enhancing families. Families that see this as a major task or focus look for every opportunity to use the important dimensions of sustainability to provide opportunities and experiences.

It is from work that we have done with this family, and others like it, that we are focused on these aspects of their development and have begun to measure and develop avenues to assist other families in exercising this muscle.

Vignette: Learning to Navigate Challenges

Jim Burke had grown up in a family that he felt did not prepare him to deal with the ups and downs of life, much less business challenges. He often thought that because of the family's resources, he had never encountered any real obstacles. When he had children, he began to think about it more and decided that his parents had often dealt with challenges for him and his siblings. Even when his brother Ralph had trouble in school, with other kids and with teachers, his mom and dad would manage to help out and make sure that Ralph did not suffer an embarrassment or negative consequence with the school. Jim learned to not do things the way that Ralph did so that he would never present such situations to his parents.

When Ralph joined him in business, Jim expected him to be a partner in the strategic planning necessary to move the family enterprise forward. Instead, he found that Ralph was easily thwarted when an obstacle was put in the way of an idea. When Jim worked up the courage to speak with him about this issue, it was interesting to hear that Ralph believed that it was an inborn characteristic that he did not have, and Jim did. After more non-judgmental discussions, they were able to think through not only what to do in the current situation but also how to help the next generation plan and develop this skill.

Case Study: The Samson Brothers Family

The Samson family prided itself on its ability to think realistically and to be proactive in its business. And so, when the opportunity came up to sell a piece of their holdings, they seized the chance, selling their residential real estate holdings while retaining their commercial real estate division. It showed great resilience on their part, taking advantage of a market turn that they saw happening, while maintaining a business unit that could provide the cash flow and capital necessary to diversify into other businesses and investments.

This shift had another impact on the family. They realized they needed to build in experiences for the next generation to help them develop resilience: to build the muscle so that they could figure out when to change direction, how to change direction, and where to go.

They started an education program where they made an agreement among all of the cousins that they would permit them to make their decisions, talk decisions through, especially around budget-ary items. If they made a mistake, deal with the mistake. They very much focused on self-reliance and self-responsibility for the next generation.

They also recognized that building resilience involved attitude, too: it called for faith and belief in each other, it called for spending time getting to know how each other interacted and did things at meetings. They talked with their grandfathers about investments and started up an investment club. They tested out ideas to see what worked and what didn't work.

They began building their resilience muscles. They invited speakers from different parts of the industry to talk about what was happening in the industry and help them to think through what they would be doing and what kinds of decisions they'd have to make as future active owners. How should they think about their portfolio of interests as a family? How do you keep to a straight line, while still allowing yourself to make right or left turns, when necessary?

Summary

Resilience, defined as the capacity of a person to absorb and overcome positive and negative disturbances, is critical to sustainability. Long-lasting family enterprises tend to be characterized by a high degree of resilience.

Resilience is not something that is innate or ingrained in family enterprises and their members: it is something that can be and must be developed (similar to a muscle); without exercise and development, the muscle ossifies. For most families, there are some inherent obstacles that can be used to develop it. However, because of their abundance of resources and the greater complexity created by the marriage of their family system to their economic one, ultra high-net-worth (UHNW) families or family enterprises generally do not face natural obstacles. This simply means that they must be more deliberate, systematic and thoughtful and must put a plan in place for developing resilience.

Resilience involves the ability to persist in the face of obstacles. It provides the methods for making agile right and left turns on the path toward sustainability, addressing those directional curves that the world tends to throw at you. Sustainable organizations of any kind need the ability to do this. It is important to know that resilience is not something one

is born with—it is something that one develops. We believe there are several kinds of opportunities that enhance all the interdependent elements of resilience.

The key or essence of resilience is that it does not change the core of the family enterprise—that core remains the same. Instead, it gives families a way or a method to meet changes in the environment and in the landscape. Families need to define their values, mission and develop the other aspects of sustainability—this will serve them well in managing the shifts. ■

---

[1] *Mind in the Making: The Seven Essential Life Skills Every Child Needs, by Ellen Galinsky, 2010.*

[2] *How to Make Stress Your Friend, (Jane McGonigal, 2017 Ted Talks) https://www.ted.com/talks/ kelly_mcgonigal_how_to_make_stress_your_friend*

9

The Future

It's customary to end a book by looking backward, wrapping up the ideas and points of the subject of the book. Rather than simply look back, I would like to use this as an opportunity to look forward.

Granted, it is a bit strange to entitle a last chapter "the future"—especially given that the book has been driven all along by an examination of sustainability, a topic that by definition is about the future. I am reminded of the topical essays one was asked to write in grade school, with this one titled, "What did I learn while writing this book and what does it imply for the future in terms of family enterprises and their sustainability?"

Whenever one writes on any topic, one expects to learn new things—and to be taken in new and unexpected directions. That's certainly been the case here: In writing this new edition, I have been spurred to think not only of the concept of sustainability but also its particular relevance for today's world and for families living in this world. I did not anticipate examining the core of what it means to be separate yet connected on the familial, community and global level. I did not anticipate what it truly means to participate in the world with a mindset of abundance yet realizing the impact of the reality of scarcity. Being generous became a much more far-reaching concept than I imagined, and the notion of gratitude became inextricably linked to generosity. While sustainability was/is the nominal focus, my own focus has never been only confined to the behaviors or practices that we typically associate with sustainability. Rather, it has also been about the idea of making a choice to continue; a choice that includes an effort to balance the focus on the internal; the needs of family members and the external; and, the family's sense of its purpose in the world.

addition to the many new things I learned
out sustainability and family enterprises, the
ocess of writing this book has also been a
rsonal journey—both an act of discovery and
-discovery for me—something that I would
e to share.

y experience with family enterprises (to-
ther with those of my colleagues) made me
owledgeable from an "advisory perspective"
to what could promote sustainability in fam-
enterprises. But to write about something
at readers will identify with and absorb and
at adds to a body of knowledge or informs it,
u have to immerse yourself in the subject
atter. And as you do so, you find that you are
ing much more than assembling or codifying
erything that you've learned to date—you
scover that it is a continuation and a deepen-
g of everything you have learned. That's
rtainly been the case with me: I have gained
great deal in developing this new edition
the book and I hope that the six learnings
elow will also be part of what a family
ight learn in the process of examining
eir sustainability.

1. Learning is in the doing, in relationship
   to what is being learned and with whom
   one is engaged in the process
2. Leadership involves, at its core, a sense
   of self in context and a belief that the
   whole is larger than the sum of the parts—
   and that to engage the whole, one must
   engage the parts
3. Keeping the balance of separateness
   and connectedness is important to
   understanding the role one plays in
   sustainability and how one contributes
   to it

4. Sustainability is something one seeks
   and something one contributes to
5. Being generous of spirit and sharing
   gratitude connects us all to our
   humanity; it provides the basis of
   a social compact
6. Sustainability changes evolution into a
   process where family has agency: the
   power and the focus to systematically
   influence how long, and how, they want
   to continue together as an economic
   unit

Lastly, I would like to address the unknowable
aspect of the future for enterprising families.

Families are always evolving: It is part and
parcel of the forward movement of time.
There are normative stages of family life, and
families move along a continuum in dealing
with them. Periodically, we see the continuum
shifting somewhat, as in the case with the
recent generational shift towards marrying
later and in people living longer. Whatever
the continuum, every family, to a greater
or lesser extent, wants to utilize current
resources in a manner that enhances what
the next generation has available.

Families who share assets can be certain that
they will evolve. But since their emotional life
also is intermeshed with their economic one,
it is critical to their survival that they be more
conscious and deliberate in their approach
to evolution. It's a circular process whereby
increased functioning in the "crossover space"
between the emotional and the economic
contributes to the increased functioning of
each family member independently and
then against the whole.

For enterprising families, it is the careful examination of what went before and where one wishes to be that marks the journey forward. Without that examination, determining the risks and opportunities becomes guesswork. If you don't know the challenges, planning for them becomes impossible.

In identifying what we know, we also identify what we do not know, enabling us to name and track forces that may impact us. Some of these may be specific to the family and some to global economy. Here are some of the key trends and forces that need to be monitored:

- Changing family demographics
- Changing views of money, success and wealth
- Democratization of information
- View of relationships

Changing family demographics

Family statistics are changing: The next generation has a different kind of footprint on and relationship to the world. The younger generations, while still retaining a local imprint, tend to view themselves as belonging more to a global community. Plus, relationships, in their view, do not rely on or require a physical presence. They exist on the internet, social media and texting. They want the freedom to move about in the world and to find their own way. With the increasing importance of internet-based economies and disruptive economic models, they also seek out new ideas and knowledge in ways their parents never knew. These new ideas may push family enterprises into new areas on the economic scene and challenge them to think more about the future of the family holdings.

Combine this with the fact that in the UHNW group, life expectancy has increased (at least among Caucasian UHNWs), and it means that family enterprises need to be able to serve and support a much larger family system with several generations and diversity in geography and cultures.

Changing views of money, success and wealth

Zip codes defining one's access to resources. Wealthy parents bribing college admissions officers to ensure that their kids get into to the most competitive and desirable universities. These and other instances of the negative impact of wealth and a celebrity-oriented culture that may be signaling a breach in our social compact of rewarding people on the basis of ability, rather than birth.

At the same time, however, such breaches may also signal a shift to a more balanced, less entitled view of wealth. The younger generation seems to be redefining what money means to them and their place in the world. They see the world as less certain but are committed to making it a better place for them and future generations. Our experience is that younger people are beginning to use their wealth to reinforce the social compact, and philanthropy has become a major way to do so. It is possible that along with these changes will come the realization that money is not the sole measure of success.

Democratization of information

It was not so long ago that when I wanted to know how to spell something or find out the meaning of a word, I had to go to my bookshelf and reach for my own trustworthy dictionary. No more. Now not only can I

et answers to any question I have immedi-
ely, but so can anyone else. No longer is
formation the "property" of a privileged
w—now everyone has access through their
mart devices. People can check economic
ata and trends in industries, employment and
obal economies. It is readily available as long
, one has the willingness to poke around on
e internet. What this also means is that
VERYONE has the same information and can
ke advantage of it in business and in life—
at is, if they also have the critical thinking/
nalytic skills to examine the information
nd make use of it in their planning.

iew of relationships

lultigenerational families used to view their
gacy as their history and something that
as their past and future—in other words, as
omething permanent. Now, legacy is viewed
; a living history, a set of values and princi-
es and a mission/vision that changes as the
mily and society changes. Relationships
 families seemed to be viewed in a similar
anner: long-lasting with few possibilities for
family member to define a point for them
 exit from the joint economy. There seems
 be a movement toward defining how entries
nd exits in the family economy can be
anaged without disturbing the essence
f either subsystem.

At the same time, the nature of relationships
in families has also been changing. There are
few families that have not experienced divorce
and/or remarriage. Gay marriage and gay
parenting have now become a part of the
family tapestry. All of these changes mean that
some additional thought needs to be given
to documents that have traditionally defined
inheritance, marriage and trusts, that is,
entrances, exits and beneficial ownership.
The full impact of the younger generation's
willingness to redefine gender and relationships remains unclear.

However, there is evidence that young people
have less of a long-term commitment to where
they work. Work itself is changing—its place
and nature in the scheme of things—and young
people are less committed to working in one
place and are frequently looking to make their
mark on the world, not necessarily in their
family enterprise. We see a beginning trend
in families to create space for creativity and
development of younger generations that
will permit them separateness as well as
connectedness.

Summary

Having begun this chapter with a discussion of the future, it seems somehow fitting to conclude with a few thoughts on the same topic. The future, as we know, is by definition unknowable and unpredictable, whether one is talking about the future prospects of an individual, a family enterprise, a nation or the planet. And it is fleeting by nature: the "future" is quickly folded into the present and soon becomes a matter of the past.

Sustainability, in our view, is a means of bringing about unity and purpose to the past, present and future of family enterprises— in part by de-emphasizing the now for the sake of the later. This is not to say that sustainability must play itself out in the same, identical way with each and every family: The sustainability journey has no single destination but rather many points of rest and recalibration.

It is our hope that this book provides families and their advisors with the opportunity to formulate a pathway—a travel alternative—that periodically can be reviewed and re-evaluated for forward progress and direction. The ability to see the alternative routes and to integrate the needed shifts will be enhanced by a family's ability to be resilient. There may need to be adjustments in speed, pacing and even objectives, but the alternative routes will always be toward sustainability. ■

Made in the USA
Middletown, DE
23 September 2023

38571952R00066